VICTORIAN PARLOUR GAMES
FOR TODAY

VICTORIAN
PARLOUR GAMES
FOR TODAY

COMPILED BY
PATRICK BEAVER

PETER DAVIES
LONDON

B

Peter Davies Ltd
15 Queen Street, Mayfair, London W1X 8BE

LONDON MELBOURNE TORONTO
JOHANNESBURG AUCKLAND

793
BEA

Printed and bound in Great Britain by
W & J Mackay Limited, Chatham
by photo-litho

FOR
JOHN BRUNEL

Eager and never weary we pursued
Our home amusements by the warm peat-fire
At evening; when with pencil and with slate,
In square divisions parcell'd out, and all
With crosses and with cyphers scribbled o'er,
We schemed and puzzled, head opposed to head
In strife too humble to be named in Verse.
Or round the naked table, snow-white deal,
Cherry or maple, sate in close array,
And to the combat, Loo or Whist, led on.

William Wordsworth, 'The Prelude' Book 1

Contents

Introduction

Satirical drawing of animals playing
a board game (Egyptian New Kingdom,
c. 3000 BC, British Museum)

ALL GAMES, from the Roman gladiatorial games of fighting to the death to a quiet round of cards or charades played in the parlour on a Sunday afternoon, are imitations of real life situations. This is equally true of physical or mental contests, games of chance or of combinations of any of these. Team games, whether played in field or parlour are all essentially exercises in combat. Games wherein the individual pits his wits against one or more other individuals are but a reflection of the struggle to live and better oneself in the world of reality. The activity of playing games is not only a means of occupying leisure time in a meaningful way; it is also the expression of an instinct, for play is far older than culture. In his book, *Homo Ludens*, Professor J. Huizinga reminds us that animals did not wait for man to teach them their playing.

1

Animals play, but, of course, they do not 'play games' for the term 'play' is, by itself, technically applicable only to informal play activities. In human beings, those activities take such forms as playing 'cowboys and Indians', playing 'hospitals', playing with dolls and toys and playing in the sand. In this form of playing there are no rules and no fixed procedure. The events follow each other spontaneously and are the result of caprice.

A *game* on the other hand, be it Blind Man's Buff, chess or polo is subject to definite rules and procedures, the infringement of which usually involves a penalty of some form, and the action of the game leads to a given climax, and this generally consists of victory for one side or person over the others. This definition applies not only to contests that require great strength, skill and endurance but also to the quieter games of the parlour.

Some indoor games of the ancient world were, like bridge and chess today, taken very seriously indeed. The Greek game of Cottabus (now unhappily extinct) had not only its professional players but also special buildings in which to accommodate players and spectators. The object of the game (which was inextricably linked with wine-drinking) was for the player to cast a portion of the wine left in his cup in such a way that, without breaking its bulk during its passage through the air, it should strike a special target and, by its impact, produce a distinct noise. This game seems to be unique insofar as the throwing about of wine is concerned although it should be mentioned that G. K.

Playing Cottabus (from a Greek urn in the
British Museum)

Chesterton and Maurice Baring used to indulge in indoor wine-throwing battles between themselves. Only port wine was used and Baring kept a special stock of inferior port for the contests which he labelled 'Throwing Port'. Two glasses were the only equipment required for, needless to say, only the port was thrown, not the bottles.

The Victorian age has been called the Golden Age of many things. It was certainly the Golden Age of the parlour game. It is true that many of these games, from Blind Man's Buff and Nine Men's Morris to Chess and Backgammon, had been played for hundreds of years – the more primitive in village inns and on village greens, the more advanced in the drawing rooms of the wealthy. But it took a large urban middle-class, deprived of the village inn, the village hall and other rural social centres, to develop and popularize the parlour game. To do this it drew on all available sources. Games like Charades and Tableaux Vivants, for years popular in the great houses of the rich, were all adapted to the suburban parlour. The ancient game of Nine Men's Morris, or Merels, once played with stones on a playing area marked on the ground, became a board game, as did Fox and Geese and many other old country pastimes.

Children's games were also adapted and developed for parlour gatherings – games whose origins were lost in antiquity but which had almost certainly evolved from religious beginnings or primitive customs and which had survived through the playing activities of children and their innate conservatism. Children possess a strong sense of the dramatic and they prefer games that involve action. It is easy to see, therefore, how games were handed down from generation to generation and changed very little in the process. The game of London Bridge is Falling Down is a good example of a primitive preoccupation with an early ritual perpetuated in a children's game. First the bridge falls down; then it is built up with sticks and stones, then with iron bars, then with silver and gold and so on until the prisoner is taken. This reflects the primitive practice of burying a human sacrifice in the foundations of certain buildings. Again, the game of Oranges and Lemons indicates a contest between opposing parties and an execution, and, although the sequence of events is not clear (for the contest takes place after the beheading), these two events are the chief factors.

Then there is the old English country game of Drop Handkerchief which, eventually, found its way into the Victorian parlour, although it lost its meaning on the way. Originally a kissing game played at spring fairs, its origins were probably connected with fertility customs, for the amatory significance of the handker-

3

chief is well known. In the *Badminton Magazine* of February 1896, a writer traces the progress of the game from country to town:

> 'Drop Handkerchief' is a pastime that has much fascination for the observer, and, happily, it may still be played with something like its pristine simplicity in country places. There the game, as of yore, is not a mere incident of an uproarious party: it is the event of the day. The girls look forward to it with trepidation and the youths with delight. The salute [kiss] is given in a ceremonious manner, it means something both to the giver and the recipient that is remembered long afterwards, and is often not without a happy result. The game, as regards its mere rules, remains the same now as it has been for hundreds of years. But the players for the most part are different, and those who witness it as played by the young men and women of London nowadays can only regret that nineteenth-century vulgarity has desecrated a pastime, venerable, but ever young, and imbued through long ages with the spirit of simple gaiety and rustic romance.

We can only regret that the twentieth century, with its passive attitude towards the spending of leisure time, has replaced most recreational activities, both for young and old, with one, single, international preoccupation – television. Even the parlour game has been swallowed up by this medium and regurgitated as a commercial operation. Not only do we have professional sport but professional chess, professional billiards, professional quizzes, and professional guessing games. Even Christmas parties, parlour games included, are beamed into homes as a substitute for the real thing, to be passively watched rather than actively engaged in by a generation of children who are in danger of forgetting how to play. (But then, what else is to be expected in a society that commemorates Christmas as a commercial binge. And, indeed, what else can we expect from a generation that has, significantly, abolished the word 'parlour', meaning 'a room for conversation', and substituted for it 'lounge' which is early nineteenth-century slang for slouch and, even earlier, a word meaning 'a sitting room in a hotel'.)

The fact that our nineteenth-century forebears did not spend all their evenings speechlessly gazing at a moving version of their magic-lantern does not mean that they were as bored as we may be when deprived of the monotonous, habit-forming, visual diet that we accept as entertainment. Hopefully a happier and more enlightened generation of the future, having rediscovered that it is satisfying for man to do things for himself, may wonder how *we* endured entire evenings gazing at coloured lights.

Apart from the occasional treatise on 'serious' games such as Whist, no book dealing with parlour games appeared until 1825. Thereafter, and up to the end of the century, hundreds of such volumes were published. A book that listed and described all the games recorded during the period would be one of encyclopaedic proportion. Ruthless pruning has therefore been the main task in compiling this book.

Several games have been omitted because they were obviously invented for a games-hungry public and, in consequence, are so trivial and tedious that it is doubtful whether they ever got beyond the covers of the books in which they appeared. One example of such a game will suffice:

> Each player is supplied with a saucer and a packet of new pins. At a signal, each player must take out all the pins, one by one, and then put them back in the holes of the paper package. The first to do so is the winner.

I cannot believe that a party of people foregathered to enjoy themselves would have wasted much time on such humdrum diversions, especially when they had at their disposal games as delightful as Wolf and Lamb, Guessing Blind Man, Queen of Sheba, The Mousetrap and Poor Pussy, as well as the various kissing games that made up a good proportion of the party-organizer's repertoire.

I have omitted games such as Tiddlywinks and Halma because the rules of play are always supplied with the equipment that is necessary for them; I have also omitted those games requiring special apparatus that is no longer available. Games such as Bridge and Chess are excluded because so much has been written on them by experts.

A number of pastimes are included that are not strictly covered by my earlier definition of what constitutes a 'game', but which are essentially party games nevertheless. I have called these 'Romps'. Those who, in their childhood, indulged in these romps at every birthday and Christmas party over the years will remember that although the whole point of each of these activities relied upon the supposed ignorance of the victim, one's excitement and pleasure was increased by the very knowledge that, as victim, one was about to be soaked with water or bumped on the floor, and one was perfectly aware of the sequence of events that would bring this 'misfortune' about.

In general, my aim has been to present a selection of old parlour games which includes something for all ages, all occasions and all tastes and I would like to thank those (children as well as adults)

5

who have helped me to make this selection. For many of the card games I am indebted to *The Cyclopaedia of Card and Table Games* (1891) by the self-styled Professor Louis Hoffman. My thanks are also due to The Bodley Head for permission to use the extract from *Frenzied Fiction* by Stephen Leacock.

1 General Party Games

IT MAY be argued that the further north one travels in Great Britain the more civilized is the society one encounters. This is a reversal of history but there it is. One of the manifestations of this phenomenon is that in northern England, the more so in Scotland, few hosts would consider a party complete (with or without children) unless it included a round or two of some of the games we offer in this chapter.

Under the heading 'General Party Games' are grouped all those games whose sole function is to produce merriment. None of them requires the slightest exercise of the intellect. Some are suitable for children, some offer fun to grown-ups, while others will be found enjoyable by companies of widely differing ages. Many of them are variations on a theme, and in such cases (Blind Man Games, for example) the original themes, well-known though they may be, are also given.

7

Some of the games have no 'point' but are merely exercises in provoking mirth. For these I make no excuse, having often witnessed the most dignified (and sober) persons laughing most heartily while playing simple games like Poor Pussy. The reader who doubts this is recommended to persuade one of his sterner friends or relations to indulge in a round of Throwing the Smile or to play The Laughing Game with a straight face. Indeed, I suspect that our grandfathers may have laughed a great deal more than we do today.

To those who criticize the prim-and-properness of the Victorians, it may come as a surprise that many of the old parlour games were merely excuses for the exchange of one, or many, amatory salutes. Perhaps such critics have been deceived by the tongue-in-cheek attitude of the Victorians themselves to such matters. Writing in 1854, the anonymous author of a popular book, *Round Games for All Parties*, remarked:

> We believe that in what a popular writer has called 'the present strict state of society and mammas', great objections exist to the introduction of 'kissing' in games. To silence them all – and to keep up that tremendously exalted tone for which our work intends to be celebrated – we hereby announce, that all games requiring the introduction of the objectionable ceremony, are intended by us to be played exclusively in family parties, consisting of brothers, sisters, maiden aunts, grandmothers and uncles. Cousins may be admitted under certain restrictions – but the privilege can extend no further. We hope none of our readers will think of breaking through this regulation. If they do, all we can say is, we can't help it. We have done our best.

In compiling this collection, I have studied scores of twentieth-century books on parlour games. Not one of the games described in all these books allows for a single kiss.

a. BLIND MAN GAMES

Blind Man's Buff: One of the party volunteers to be the first blind man, or is chosen by lot. A handkerchief or scarf is tied over his eyes and he is turned round three times. He then tries to catch any other player he can. The other players tease him by pushing him, pulling at his clothes, tickling his face with a feather etc. When he succeeds in seizing someone the blind man has to guess who it is. If he is right his prisoner becomes the blind man. In another version known as French Blind Man's Buff the blind man's hands are tied behind his back and he is only permitted to

walk backwards; he captures his prisoner by touching him. The word 'Buff' is Middle English for a blow or buffet.

The Bellman: In this version of Blind Man's Buff *everybody* is blindfolded except one player. He carries a small bell which he rings from time to time. There is much colliding and seizing of one blind man by another. The blind man who catches the bell-man changes places with him. This game is derived from a much earlier one once played at country fairs in which a belled pig took the place of the player with the bell.

Guessing Blind Man: The company seat themselves on chairs forming a circle with the blind man in the centre. He is turned round three times during which manoeuvre the rest of the players all change seats. The blind man then walks forward and sits on the lap of the first person he contacts and tries to guess who it is. Should he fail after three attempts he pays three forfeits (*see* Chapter 6). If he guesses the second time he pays but one forfeit. According to a handbook of parlour games published in 1844, the blind man (when it *was* a man) always endeavoured, through a little preliminary probing, to choose a lady's lap on which to sit but 'a good deal of fun is caused by a young lady throwing her skirt over the lap of the gentleman next to her'. This would be difficult today. Should the blind man guess on his first attempt, the person discovered takes his place, otherwise a new blind man is chosen. There is another variety to this game in which the blind man says to the lap's owner 'Can you guess?', which the person asked must repeat. Otherwise the rules remain the same.

Buff with the Wand: In this variant of the time-honoured game, the blinded person, stick in hand, stands in the centre of the room. The rest of the party join hands in a ring around him and dance to music. When the music stops the blind man brings his stick down upon one of the circle who is then required to grasp its end. The blind one then makes any sound he likes – a street cry, the sound of an animal or anything else – which the captured person must imitate. Should the blind man guess who holds the stick he passes the blindfold to the person caught. If not he must keep the bandage and try again.

Blind Postman: First, a postmaster-general and a postman are appointed. The room furniture is pushed to one side to make space for movement and the company arrange themselves around the sides of the room. The postmaster-general then tours the room and writes down the players' names together with the name of a town for each person. The blindfolded postman is then placed in the middle of the room and the postmaster announces that a letter has been sent from one town to another – say from London to Glasgow. The representatives of these two cities then stand up and as quietly as possible change seats. As they do this the postman attempts to secure one of the seats himself. If he succeeds the former occupant of that seat takes on the job of Blind Postman.

Cat and Mouse: The players sit in two rows facing each other with enough space between the rows to allow one person to pass through. Two are selected as cat and mouse, both of whom are blindfolded. They are placed one at each end of the pathway and may walk around each of the two rows of spectators but must keep within touching distance of them. The object is for the cat to catch the mouse – the hunt being conducted entirely by ear. When the mouse has been caught, another cat and mouse are chosen.

Alice, Where Art Thou? Each gentleman is given a lady for a partner – *not*, be it noted, the lady of his choice. The gentlemen are then sent out of the room and blindfolded while, in the meantime, the ladies move away from their former positions. The men then return and try to locate their partners. The men may talk but the ladies may not. The winner is the one who first finds his partner. A variation on this game is to give each lady an animal's name and to permit her to use the call of that creature twice to aid her partner in his search.

Animals: All the players except the blind man station themselves in different parts of the room. The blind man then feels his way around until he touches somebody. That player must at once give an imitation of the noise made by some animal – donkey, cat, dog, cow, pig, cock, repeating it up to three times if requested. The blind man must then guess the name of his prisoner and if he does so the person named becomes blind man.

Blind Man's Steps: This game, although childishly simple, can be very funny. The blindfolded player is placed in the middle of the room and asked whom he would like to capture (or to kiss). He is then turned to face the object of his choice and told how many steps he must take to make contact. He then inevitably makes absurd mistakes in the direction and the length of the steps he must take.

11

Isaac and Rebecca: The players, holding hands, form a ring, in which stand Isaac and Rebecca, both blindfolded. Every time he calls out, 'Rebecca, where art thou?' she has to reply, 'Isaac, here I am,' and he endeavours to catch her by following her voice.

Squeak Piggy Squeak: All the players but one sit on chairs in a circle facing inwards. The odd player is placed in the middle of the ring, blindfolded and given a cushion. Holding the cushion in front of him with both hands the blindfolded player must find a lap by feeling with the cushion, and then, placing it on the lap, sit on it saying 'Squeak, piggy, squeak.' He may demand three squeaks before attempting to identify the piggy. If he is wrong he must try another lap and go through the same procedure. If and when he succeeds in identifying the piggy, the identified player takes the blindfold and cushion and the game is resumed.

b. GAMES WITH CHAIRS

Musical Chairs: A number of chairs (one less than the number of players) is placed in a row, facing alternately in opposite directions. The players march around the chairs in time to music and when the music stops every player endeavours to find a seat. The unlucky player without a chair drops out of the game, one more chair is removed and the game is restarted. Players are not allowed to touch any chair during the march-around. The player who captures the very last remaining chair is the winner.

Musical Potatoes: This is Musical Chairs played without chairs. The players sit in a circle on the floor all but one holding a potato in his right hand and behind his back. Music is started and each player passes his potato to the player on his left. When the music stops, the player *without* a potato in his hand is eliminated. One potato is also withdrawn from the game which then continues on the same principles as musical chairs.

Caterpillar: As many chairs as there are players are placed in a circle in the middle of the room all facing inwards. All the players except one seat themselves, while the odd player stands in the middle of the circle. When all the others are settled, the odd man tries to sit down on the vacant chair. This the other players try to prevent by moving onto it – first in one direction then in the other, so that at one moment the vacant seat may be almost within the odd player's touch and at the next at the very opposite side of the circle. If the seated players move from chair to chair quickly enough, it will be some time before the odd man can sit down. When he does it is the player on his *left* who takes his place. A most energetic and hilarious game.

Numbers: A number of chairs equal to the number of players is placed in a row. The players seat themselves and are numbered off from left to right. The seats retain these numbers throughout the game. The player seated at the head of the row, i.e. he who is number 'one', calls out another number, say 'five'. 'Five' must immediately respond by calling out another number and so on. When a person does not immediately respond to his number he must go to the foot of the row; all the other players moving up one to make room for him and in so doing changing their numbers. Thus 'seven' becomes 'six' and so forth down the line. The length of game is governed either by a time-limit or by limiting the number of calls. The player at the head of the row when the game ends is the winner.

Change Seats, the King's Come: As many chairs are placed around the room as will accommodate all the players save one. The seat-less one is chosen by lot. When all the rest are seated, the one without a seat stands in the middle and says, 'Change seats, change seats, change seats, change seats' as many times as he likes, while all the others remain on the alert for him to add 'the King's come'. At this, all the seated players must change seats but *not* with a neighbour and the caller tries to obtain a seat for himself. The principal player may sometimes say instead 'The King's *not* come' and if he uses this device with some skill he

13

can cause great confusion as some of the players attempt to change seats while others remain seated. This confusion makes it much easier for him to capture a chair, leaving another player standing to call 'Change seats'. This is a good version of musical chairs when no music is available. Sir Walter Scott mentions this ancient game in *Rob Roy:* 'Here auld ordering and counter-ordering – but patience! patience! – We may ae day play at *Change seats, the king's coming.*'

Sea and Fishes: The company seat themselves in a circle of chairs leaving one player out who represents the 'Sea'. The other players having each taken the name of a fish, the 'Sea' walks around the circle calling out the names of the fishes one by one. Each player, on hearing his adopted name called out, rises and follows the sea. When *all* have thus been called (and the Sea may have some difficulty in remembering the fish-names of all the players), the Sea begins to run about crying, 'The Sea is troubled! The Sea is troubled!' The other players still follow until the Sea suddenly sits down, an example that must immediately be followed by all the other players. The one who fails to secure a seat becomes the 'Sea' and the game continues.

How Do You Like Your Neighbours? The company must seat themselves around the room leaving plenty of space in the middle in which to move about. One person is left standing in the centre and starts the game by asking any other player, 'How do you like your neighbours?' The answer must be either 'Not at all' or 'Very much'. Should the reply be 'Not at all' the player is asked what other two members of the company he or she would prefer as neighbours and these must immediately change places with the unwanted ones. During the change the questioner must try to secure one of the vacated seats and leave one of the four as the next questioner. If the answer is 'Very much' then *all* the company must change seats leaving one as the interrogator.

c. HUNTING GAMES

Hunt the Slipper: All the players but one sit on the floor in a circle with their legs crossed, one acting as Chief, and all pretending to mend shoes. The odd player brings a slipper to the Chief Cobbler and asks for it to be mended saying:

> Cobbler, cobbler, mend my shoe,
> Get it done by half-past two.

14

After turning his back for a moment, the slipper hunter demands its return but is told that it has been lost. He then starts to search for it. The Cobblers all place their hands beneath their knees and pass the slipper secretly from one to the other while the slipper hunter can demand to see the hands of any one cobbler at any time until he finds it. The last holder of the slipper then becomes its owner.

Hunt the Thimble: All the company leave the room except the thimble hider who places the thimble in a place where it can be seen without moving other objects. The players then enter the room all together and walk around hunting the thimble. No word is spoken but when anyone sees the thimble he sits down without indicating where it is. The last player to sit down pays a forfeit.

Hunt the Ring: A ring or a small key is threaded onto a long piece of string which is then fastened to form a circle. The company then stand in a circle all holding the string and pass the ring from hand to hand whilst the hunter, standing in the middle, endeavours to guess in whose hand the ring is. It is, of course, only passed behind the hunter's back. Whoever is caught with the ring takes his place in the middle of the circle.

Hot Boiled Beans: One player is sent out of the room and a small article is hidden. This being done the absent player is told, 'Hot Boiled Beans and Bacon for supper, hurry up before it gets cold.'

On hearing this the player returns to the room and searches for the missing article while the rest of the company inform him that his supper is getting 'very cold', 'cold', 'warmer', 'hot', 'very hot' or 'burning' according to how far or near he is from the article to be found.

d. GUESSING GAMES

Who Am I? Each player in turn secretly assumes the identity of a famous person, living or dead. It is the task of the others to discover this identity by asking questions. The 'celebrity' must only answer 'Yes' or 'No'.

Q. Are you a man?
A. No.
Q. Are you living?
A. No.
Q. Are you an actress?

And so on until the identity is discovered as being Florence Nightingale, Lucrezia Borgia, Helen of Troy, Anne Boleyn or who have you.

A variant of this game demands that one player leaves the room while the rest of the company invest him with an identity. He then returns and the game proceeds in reverse as it were, the 'celebrity' asking the company 'Am I a man?' etc.

Yes or No: In this game one person leaves the room while the remainder fix upon an object word for him to discover. On being recalled he may ask any number of questions to try to discover the word but the answers given him must be simply 'Yes' or 'No' – nothing more.

Another version of this game simply reverses the procedure. One of the company, without leaving the room, thinks of an object to be guessed at by the remainder of those present. Again, he may only answer 'Yes' or 'No'.

The Object Game: This is a variation of the game now famous as *Twenty Questions* and is more suitable than the latter when a party of twelve or more are playing. The party is divided into two equal teams. One person from each team is sent outside and between them they decide on the object that the others must guess. The company then arrange themselves in two distinct circles far enough away from one another to prevent the remarks of one side being overheard by the other. The two representatives then take their places within the respective circles and a race begins to discover the secret word. The rules of the game stipulate that the number of questions each side may ask should be limited to twenty though usually it is impossible to enforce this without two other players acting as referees. One rule however must be strictly adhered to and that is that the answers given to the questioners are limited to 'Yes' or 'No'. If a question is asked that cannot be answered with a simple positive or negative then it must not be answered at all. The team that arrives at the correct word first is, of course, the winning one.

How, Why, When and Where: One player thinks of the name of an object – any object – it being the task of the other players to discover what it is by asking (only once) the following four questions:

> How do you like it?
> Why do you like it?
> When do you like it?
> Where do you like it?

The first player is entitled to think of a word that has more than one meaning and to confuse his questioners by using all those meanings in his reply. Thus – male (masculine), mail (letters) and mail (armour):

How do you like it? When it's a good friend.
Why do you like it? Because it sometimes brings good news.
When do you like it? First thing in the morning.
Where do you like it? In a museum.

Throwing Up Lights: In this game two players secretly decide upon a word and then carry on a conversation between themselves which will throw some light upon what the word is. The object of the game is for the other players to guess the word by listening to the conversation. If a player thinks that he has discovered the word, he calls out 'I strike a light,' and then whispers his guess into the ear of one of the leaders. If he has guessed correctly he joins in the conversation and the remaining players continue to try to detect the word. If on the other hand he has mistaken the word he must sit on the floor with a handkerchief over his face until the end of the game or until he guesses the word correctly.

Smells: This game needs to be prepared beforehand. A number of small vessels – cups, glasses or jam-jars – each contain one

17

substance that gives off an odour. A piece of boot polish, some vinegar, some paraffin oil, a piece of apple, some custard powder – the list of available substances is almost endless. Needless to say, substances such as orange, petrol, ammonia etc. which have highly characteristic odours should not be used. The players are sent out of the room and one by one they re-enter to be blindfolded. Each dish is then presented to the player's nose and he must guess what it contains. When his attempts are finished he stays to watch the fun as the other members of the party try their luck – and luck it usually is as will be demonstrated to any who play this game. Strawberry jam, for instance, can, when not seen, be quite easily mistaken for cleaning fluid, lemonade or even brilliantine.

A modern version of this game is to pre-record onto tape a number of common sounds and to use these instead of 'smells'. I think the original game is far better.

Recognition: For this game a prepared list of objects is required. It can either be duplicated beforehand according to the number of expected players or the list may be dictated to the players, each of whom will write it down. The players must, within a time limit, record what famous person, mythical, fictional or historical, each object suggests. A possible list might be as follows:

A burnt cake	King Alfred
A muddy cloak	Sir Walter Raleigh
A lighthouse	Grace Darling
A burning bush	Moses
A footprint in the sand	Robinson Crusoe
A glass slipper	Cinderella
A parrot	Long John Silver
Long hair	Samson
Wet feet	King Canute
A magic sword	King Arthur
A round table	King Arthur

The list can, of course, be varied to suit the average age of the party.

Stool of Repentance: One member of the party is sent out of the room while the rest each make a criticism of him or her. These are noted down by one of the players. A stool or chair is set up in the middle of the room and the penitent is called in and stood upon it. The criticisms are then read out to him one by one, thus: 'Somebody says you are conceited – who?' and the victim has to guess the name of his critic. Then he is told that someone considers him greedy or ugly and so on. If he guesses a sufficient (pre-arranged) number of his critics he is absolved and joins the circle for the next round; otherwise he pays a forfeit and in theory should undergo the ordeal again but as the game ceases to be amusing if the same person is twice dealt with he is usually considered to have earned his release whether he guesses correctly or not.

Shadow Buff: A large white sheet is pinned against a wall of the room while on a table some distance away from it, a bright light is placed. One player sits on the floor facing the sheet, with his back to the light. All other lights in the room being extinguished the remainder of the company pass one by one behind the watcher who has to identify each by his shadow. Gestures may be used, masks or false noses worn, in fact any device may be employed to confuse the guesser. Those whose identity is successfully discovered must pay a forfeit.

e. CHASING AND CATCHING GAMES

The Wolf and the Lambs: This is a game which is best described in the words of the Victorian author of *Round Games for All Parties:*

> In this game, all the ladies of a company may participate, but only one gentleman at a time – who should be a man of dauntless courage and great powers of endurance. This latter personage is called the *Wolf*. The principal lady takes the part of the *Shepherdess*. The others stand behind her in single file, and constitute the *Flock*. The aim of the Wolf is to catch the innocent lamb who may happen to be at the extremity of the flock. He, however, manifests his hostile intentions by the following terrible announcement! 'I am the Wolf! the Wolf! Come to eat you all up.' The Shepherdess replies, 'I am the Shepherdess, and will protect my lambs.' The Wolf retorts, 'I'll have the little white one with the golden hoofs!'
>
> The dialogue concluded, the Wolf attempts to make an irruption in the line of the flock. But the Shepherdess, extending her arms, bars his passage. If he succeeds in breaking through, the lamb placed at the end abandons her post before he can catch her, and places herself in front of the Shepherdess, where she incurs no risk; and so on with the others in succession, till the Shepherdess finds herself the last of the row. The game then finishes. The unlucky Wolf pays as many forfeits as he has allowed lambs to escape him. If, on the contrary, he has contrived to seize one of them, he does not eat her, but has the privilege of saluting [kissing] her and compels her to pay a forfeit.

This game, in company with cricket, skittles, steeplechasing and others, is more adapted to the open air than the precincts of an expensively furnished drawing-room.

Hare and Hound: The players stand in a circle in twos, one behind the other. Two are left out, the Hare and the Hound and the game is for the Hound to catch the Hare who runs around the circle until, when he chooses, he can stand in front of one of the pairs, thereby making it a three. As soon as he does this the back one of the three becomes the Hare and must run away from the Hound. The Hound must continue chasing each successive Hare until he catches one but must not touch him if he is standing in front of another. If caught, the Hare, of course, must become the Hound.

Frog in the Middle: One player sits on the floor with his legs under him; the others form a ring around. Then they prod, push or pull the frog who tries to catch one of them without rising from the floor or changing his position in the centre of the ring. The one that is caught becomes the frog.

I Wrote a Letter to My Love or *Kiss in the Ring:* All except one of the party form a ring and hold hands. The player left outside the ring walks round, touching each of the players with a handkerchief while chanting the following lines:

> I wrote a letter to my love,
> But on the way I dropped it.
> One of you has picked it up,
> And put it in your pocket.

Having selected one of the circle, the player drops the handkerchief behind him and runs round the ring. The player behind whom the handkerchief has been dropped leaves his place and tries to catch the postman before he can occupy the vacant space in the circle. The two players can dart under the uplifted arms of the other players, and sometimes the circle may obstruct either the hunter or the hunted. If the postman is not caught before he occupies the vacant space the chaser becomes the postman and the game recommences. If caught the postman gives a forfeit. Elworthy (*West Country Words*) in describing this game says:

> The person behind whom the handkerchief is dropped is entitled to kiss the person who dropped it, if he or she can catch him or her, before the person can get round the ring to the vacant place. Of course, when a girl drops it she selects a favoured swain, and the chase is severe up to a point, but when a girl is the pursuer there often is a kind of donkey race lest she should have to give the kiss which the lad takes no pains to avoid.

Kiss in the Ring, or a version of it, was forbidden by a statute of Edward IV, who, no doubt, had his reasons.

Hand in Hand out: This is a similar game to the preceding one. It is played by young people who form a circle, whereupon one of them, chosen by lot, walks around the band and, if a boy, strikes a girl, or, if a girl, strikes a boy. Then, the striker and the struck run in pursuit of each other until the latter is caught and becomes the striker for the next round.

Moving Statues or *Grandmother's Footsteps:* This game can be played indoors although it is better in a garden. One player stands at the end of the room (or lawn) and the other players have to advance on him while his back is turned. He may turn round suddenly at whatever intervals he likes and when he does so the other players must immediately become petrified. Any of them detected making the slightest movement must go back to the starting line and begin again. The first person who gets near enough to touch 'he' is the winner and, if the game is to be continued, himself becomes 'he'.

f. 'BE SERIOUS' GAMES

Throwing the Smile: The players sit round in a circle and *one* of them smiles for a moment or so. He then wipes his hand across his face to wipe off the smile and pretends to throw it to another player of his choice who has to catch it with his hand, put it on, wear it for a while and wipe it off to throw to someone else. Anyone who smiles out of turn is out and the last player remaining wins the game. Those players who are 'out' will laugh heartily as the game proceeds, thus making it more and more difficult for the remaining players to stay 'in'.

Poor Pussy: All the players sit in a circle except 'Pussy'. When all are seated, Pussy walks around on hands and knees and adopts a begging posture at the feet of one of the circle. Pussy looks as pathetic as possible and gives a pitiful 'miaow'. The one appealed to must say 'Poor Pussy' in as consoling a way as possible but without the shadow of a smile. This is repeated three times and if a smile appears on either face, a forfeit is paid and Pussy and the other player change places.

The Laughing Game: The players seat themselves in a circle and the first player begins the game by saying 'Ha'. The next player must say 'Ha, ha,' and the third, 'Ha, ha, ha.' All must be pronounced with the utmost solemnity and any player exhibiting the faintest sign of hilarity is expelled from the circle with a forfeit to his name. This game is particularly pointless for the entire circle is usually doubled up before 'Ha, ha, ha' is reached.

Buff Says Baff: This is the oldest of all the 'no laughing' games for it is mentioned as being ancient in a book of parlour games published in the 1850s. One of the company leaves the room on a supposed visit to Buff. He returns carrying a broomstick (or umbrella) and is asked by the company:

> 'Where do you come from?'
> 'From Buff!'
> 'Did he say anything to you?'
> 'Buff said, "Baff!"'
> And he gave me this staff,
> Telling me neither to smile nor laugh,
> Buff says Baff to all his men,
> And I say Baff to you again,
> And he neither laughs nor smiles,
> In spite of all your cunning wiles
> But carries his face with a very good grace
> And passes his stick to the very next place.'

The stick is then passed to another player and so on. Any player from Buff who so much as smiles during this performance has to pay a forfeit.

Pinch Without Laughing: In this extremely simple game each player pinches the nose of his neighbour, who must submit to the operation without laughing. If he so much as smiles he pays a forfeit. The nose-pinchers are permitted to use all their comic ingenuity in the attempt to induce the pinchee to lose his gravity. One writer on this intriguing game comments:

> We have heard of some designing persons blacking their finger and thumb with burnt cork, which leaves a very agreeable impression on the pinched nose. If two or three unsuspecting

23

individuals happen to be victimized in this way, they laugh
heartily *at each other*, neither suspecting that he is an object
of equal ridicule – which is not only a fine moral lesson, but
also leads to a great accumulation of forfeits.

Botany Bay: One player, taking the part of the sailor, asks the
others a question, one by one. The answer must always be 'Pork
and greens' and the first question is always: 'Here comes an old
sailor from Botany Bay. What have you got to give him today?'
The rest of the questions are entirely at the old sailor's discretion,
his object being to make the answering player laugh because of
the reply 'Pork and greens.' For example, 'What's your name?',
'What would you like for your birthday?' etc. A smile or a laugh
means a forfeit must be given.

Statues: The players dance around the room in couples with some
degree of abandon to music which will suddenly stop. When it
does all the dancers must immediately remain stock-still no
matter what their attitude may be. Any player who moves or
even smiles is disqualified until in the end only one couple remains.

The Sculptor: One player acting as the sculptor arranges all the
other players into various postures – the more absurd the better.
These postures must be retained without movement. The sculptor
then goes round to each person, endeavouring to make them laugh
or smile while they must remain absolutely immobile. He may
resort to any device to create mirth or movement short of touching anyone. The first player to move or laugh gives up a forfeit
and himself becomes the sculptor.

g. TALKING GAMES

Black-cap and Red-cap: This old game relies for its fun on the
quickness of the questioner and the other players, as questions
and answers must follow each other with great rapidity.
   The questioner gives the name of a cap of a particular colour
to all the other players, such as Black-cap, Red-cap, Blue-cap,
Yellow-cap and so on. The players then sit in a row on the floor
with the questioner in front of them. Each cap, on hearing his
name mentioned, either by the questioner or one of the other
players, must instantly start to his feet and answer under pain of
forfeit. All players must use the appropriate language; the omission of the prefix 'sir' or 'madam' as the case may be involves a

severe forfeit as does the slightest variation in the form of the answers. The game proceeds thus:

> *Questioner* (looking severe): What's this? Somebody's been at the strawberries! Can you tell me who it was, Red-cap?
> *Red-cap* (on his feet): Yes, sir; it was Blue-cap.
> *Blue-cap* (starting up): Who sir? I, sir?
> *Questioner:* Yes, sir; don't you hear, sir?
> *Blue-cap:* Oh no, sir; not me, sir; it was Yellow-cap.
> *Yellow-cap:* Who, sir? I, sir?

The game continues until all the players but one have fallen out through making a mistake.

The Prince of Paris: This is a variation of the preceding game. All the players are given a number from 1 upwards and one other player takes the lead. Standing in front he says, 'The Prince of Paris has lost his hat. Did you find it Number Six, sir?' Number Six must now stand up and answer, 'What, sir! I, sir?'

> *Leader:* Yes, sir! You, sir!
> *No. Six:* Not I, sir!
> *Leader:* Who then, sir?
> *No. Six:* Number One, sir!
> *No. One* (getting up): What, sir! I, sir?
> *Leader:* Yes, sir! You, sir!
> *No. One:* Not I, sir!
> *Leader:* Who then, sir?
> *No. One:* Number Eight, sir! (and so on)

The rules and penalties of the game are identical to those of Black-cap and Red-cap.

Priest cap: Yet another version of Black-cap. All the players sit in a line and each is given a number – one, two, three etc. – each keeping that number throughout the game. The Priest then says, 'I call upon Number 7', or whatever number he likes, and Number 7 must answer 'Not I, sir' before the Priest can count five. If he fails to do so he must go to the bottom of the line, but if he answers in time, the Priest asks him, 'Who then?', to which Number 7 must reply some other number, and the number thus called goes through the same process. The idea of the game is for the ladies to get all the men at the bottom of the row, while the men do their best to send the ladies there. The difficulty, of course, is in remembering the numbers of all the others. For instance, if Number 7, in answer to the question, 'Who then?', gives the number of the one already at the end of the row, he must take the bottom place himself. If the game is played quickly it is very exciting.

The Mousetrap: This is a delightful game and the description we found of it in *Round Games for All Parties* is so evocative that no apology is offered for quoting it at some length.

To play this game, there should be an equal number of ladies and gentlemen. They seat themselves in two ranks, at some distance apart, facing each other. The gentlemen are the *rats*, and the ladies the *mice*.

To each rat is allotted a word, to the mention of which he must reply by a sign or gesture agreed on. For instance, one will answer to *bread*, another to *bacon*, a third to *cheese*, and a fourth to *leather*. When either of these words is pronounced, the rat to whom it belongs must raise one hand in the air. The mice will respond – one to the word *candles*, the second to *corn*, the third to *flour*, and the fourth to *filberts*. *T*heir sign of recognition is to scratch with a key, or any other instrument, against something that will give a grating sound. When the master pronounces the word *mice*, all the mice scratch. When he says *rats*, all the rats raise their hands (*both hands* this time); forfeits being exacted for every omission.

In addition to the master of the house (who is the only one allowed to speak), there is also a *cat*, who is not seated with the other players, but concealed in a distant corner. The cat is known by the remarkable and uncommon name of *Puss*. When the master pronounces the word *cat*, our feline friend must immediately 'mew'; when the word is *puss*, he must vary his amusement by 'purring'. There is another corner, called the *Mousetrap*, to which all players caught by the cat are conducted, and thrown into durance vile. The manner of capture, and the remaining rules of the game will be seen from the following example.

The Master
(*He may say whatever he pleases, but it must be on the following model*):
Holloa! somebody has been nibbling at my *candles*.
(The Mouse bearing the name 'Candles' scratches, or pays a forfeit.)
The Master: Some *mice* have been here–(all the M I C E scratch)– or *rats*. (The RATS raise their hands – *both* hands.) I must look after the *cat*. – (PUSS mews without showing himself, or pays a forfeit.)
Puss: Mew! miaow!

26

(At the CAT's voice, all the RATS and MICE must get up alarmed, and crouch behind their chairs till the MASTER resumes.)

The Master: I don't see him anywhere about. (All reseat themselves.) I must find him, however, and shut him up here. He'll soon stop their fun. Puss! Puss!

(The CAT comes forward purring. All the RATS and MICE get up alarmed at the appearance of the common enemy, and change places – the RATS taking those of the MICE, and vice versa. The CAT darts from his corner during the movement, and tries to catch hold of one of the players before the latter can get to a seat. If he catches one standing, or seated in the rank where he or she ought not to be, the defaulter is seized and pays a forfeit.)

The Master: Off with him (or her) to the *mousetrap*!

(At this word all the other RATS and MICE bury their faces in their hands, and the CAT conducts his prisoner to the MOUSETRAP, where he remains until a fresh one is captured when he is liberated and returns to the seat newly vacated.)

The Master continues: Heyday! They've been at my *bacon* too! – (the RAT, fixed on as the disciple of 'Bacon', raises his hand) – and at my *flour*! – (The MOUSE, 'Flour', scratches) – and there's scarcely a morsel of *cheese* left! (The RAT, 'Cheese', raises his hand.) I must call that *cat* again.

Puss (concealed): Mew! miaow!

(RATS and MICE hide as before.)

The Master: Come here, puss!

Puss (approaching): Purr! Purr!

(Change of places, and pursuit, repeated.)

The Master: And here's a nice hole in the *bread*! – (the RAT, 'Bread', raises his hand) – and my nice stock of *filberts* – and now I look again at the *cheese* – (the MOUSE, 'Filberts', scratches; the RAT, 'Cheese', raises his hand). Etc.

The above will give a sufficient idea of the conduct of the game, which, played by a sufficient number of persons in an open space where seats can be at some distance from each other and where noise is of no particular consideration, will give rise to amusement of a lively description.

The Birdcatcher: This game is an ideal one for families who live in detached houses and where the baby sleeps on the top floor. A Birdcatcher is appointed who takes his place in the middle of a circle, the members of which have each taken the name of a bird – Goose, Tom-tit, Eagle, Parrot, Wren, Duck, Canary etc.

The selection of a species is entirely optional, except there *must* be an Owl in the aviary.

The Birdcatcher tells a story, introducing the names of the various birds as frequently as possible. Every bird, when its name is mentioned, must immediately make the cluck, crow, screech, chirrup or splutter peculiar to his species, the slightest mistake or delay being punished by a forfeit. So long as the Owl is not mentioned all the players sit with their hands resting on their knees. At the first mention of the Owl's name, all players must immediately put their hands *behind* their backs to avoid one of them being caught by the Birdcatcher who is wandering around inside the circle awaiting his opportunity. If, after mentioning the Owl, the Birdcatcher succeeds in seizing a hand not hidden behind its owner's back, that player pays a forfeit and changes places with the Birdcatcher.

If, on the other hand, the Birdcatcher fails to make a capture, *he* pays a forfeit and continues his narrative but the hands remain behind their owners' backs until the first bird's name is pronounced at which *all* hands return to knees – but not until then. (A sharp Birdcatcher will probably name the Owl twice running. No notice should be taken of the second mention.) The Owl is not exempt from the common rules. When his name is mentioned he must give *his* cry as well as putting his hands behind him.

Should the Birdcatcher mention 'all the birds of the air', then all give their respective cries at once. Any bird neglecting to do so, or uttering the wrong cry by mistake, pays a forfeit, as must the Birdcatcher himself if he mentions a bird not in the collection.

The following is a list of most of the birds available for this game, with their various modes of expression:

COCK	Cock-a-doodle-doo
CANARY	Pretty Dick, Pretty Dick
TURKEY	Gobble-obble-obble
MAGPIE	Jack wants his dinner
SPARROW	Chip, chip
DUCK	Quack, quack
CURLEW	Pe-wit, pe-wit
PARROT	Pretty Polly, pretty Polly
CROW	Caw, caw
OWL	To-whit, to-whit, to-whoo
GOOSE	Hiss-s-s-s
RAVEN	Cr-a-ak

Some of these may be varied. The Parrot may express himself with a facetious remark; the Raven may say 'Never more!' Any such variations, however, must be established at the start of play and strictly adhered to.

The Sportsman and the Game: This is a simpler version of the Birdcatcher. The players take the names of different birds and beasts of the field such as Hare, Rabbit, Fox, Partridge, Quail, Woodcock, Boar, Stag, Wolf, Lion etc.

One of the party takes the part of the Sportsman and tells a story in which he introduces sporting terms, names of implements, etc., to which, when mentioned, the different types of game reply by the following phrases:

The Gun:	*All* the players cry, 'Look out, look out.'
Greyhound:	The Hare says, 'Run, run.'
Terrier:	The Rabbit says, 'To earth, to earth.'
The Snare:	The Wolf *and* the Fox say, 'Not if I know it!'
The Nets:	The Lion and *all* the Birds say, 'Don't you wish you may get it?' ['You'll be lucky!']
A Thicket:	The Boar says, 'Mind my tusks.'
Staghound:	The Stag says, 'I have good legs.'
The Horn:	The Stag *and* Fox say, 'Be alive!'
The Bag:	All drop their heads on their chests as if killed – except the Lion, Stag and Boar who exclaim, 'Who's afraid!'

Any player making a mistake in word or action pays a forfeit.

Family Coach: This must be a very old game indeed for its antiquity is remarked upon in many early Victorian compendiums of games. It appears and re-appears over the decades and has recently been included in a book of indoor games under the name of Family Car. The coach version is given here. Each person takes the name of a character in a story that is improvised; they also take the name of a part of the family coach. One person stands up and tells the story and as the names or parts are mentioned the different people holding these names must stand up, turn around and sit down again. Whenever the 'Family Coach' is mentioned the entire company must rise and change seats while the teller of the story tries to secure a seat for himself, leaving the odd man out to continue the story.

The following version of the game is from *Endless Mirth* by Charles Gilbert (1864).

Dramatis Personae of the Family Coach

Mr Wiggins	THE BOX
Mrs Wiggins	RUMBLE-TUMBLE
Aunt Ellen	AXLE-TREE

Miss Jemima	SPRINGS
Captain Tobacco	DOOR
Master Harry	WHEELS
Coachman	WINDOWS
Juba	PERCH
Chloe	STEPS
The Horses	REINS
The Little Dog	WHIP
Etc., Etc.	

The Tale

A party of pleasure had agreed to go from London to visit
Richmond. The party consisted of Mr and Mrs Wiggins, Aunt
Ellen, Master Harry, Miss Jemima and Captain Tobacco. It
was proposed by Mr Wiggins, in order that they might see the
country better, that they should all travel together in the
FAMILY COACH, and Mr Wiggins soon arranged that he
and Mrs Wiggins, Aunt Ellen, her dear little dog, Miss Jemima
and Captain Tobacco should take their seats inside, whilst
Master Harry should ride on the box with the Coachman, and
Juba and Chloe, the two black servants, should take their
places in the rumble-tumble. All being perfectly satisfied with
Mr Wiggins's arrangement, the luggage was speedily packed
under the box and beneath the rumble-tumble whilst a few
more articles belonging to Aunt Ellen and Miss Jemima were
carefully stowed away in the seat of the FAMILY COACH.
Everything was ready; Juba flung open the door, the steps
were let down, the windows shut, the ladies took their seats,
the Coachman took the reins and mounted the box with
Harry by his side. 'All right!' cried Captain Tobacco, and off
they would have gone in half a twinkling had not Aunt Ellen
called out, 'But where's the Little Dog?' Search being made,
Juba soon found him rolled up under the rumble-tumble; Chloe
pulled him out and he was forthwith placed under the special
care of Aunt Ellen inside the FAMILY COACH. (And so
forth. The original version here left unfinished runs into 3,000
words.)

The Artist: This belongs to the same family as The Mousetrap and
The Birdcatcher. One player takes the part of the Artist, the rest
of the company are colours, each taking a name – blue, green,
orange etc. When a player hears his own colour mentioned he
must respond by naming another colour. In addition there are
four words that are answered by all the company: If the artist

mentions the word *colours*, all say, 'Here we are'. If he says *pencil*, they say, 'Brush! brush!' If he speaks of his *palette*, they answer with 'Colours! colours!' and if he names *turpentine*, the colours show signs of alarm and cry out, 'Help! help!' Finally, any colour named by another colour must reply, 'Here, sir.' Mistakes or hesitations are, as usual, punished by forfeits. The example we give is one hundred years old.

> *Artist:* I am commissioned by my noble patron the Marquis of Carabas, to paint a picture of the *finding of the body of Harold*. It is a very important matter. I have made my design, and shall now commence setting my palette.
> *All the Colours:* Colours! colours!
> *Artist:* I intend to astonish the critics by the brilliancy of my colours.
> *All:* Here we are!
> *Artist:* I can't employ you all at a time – rather a task for a single pencil.
> *All:* Brush! brush!
> *Artist:* Silence! or I'll exterminate you with a dose of turpentine.
> *All:* Help! help!
> *Artist:* I'll begin with the eyes of the fair Edith. They ought to be black. (If the Artist names a colour not in the collection, he pays a forfeit. The same rule applies to the Colours.)
> *Black:* Green! green!
> *Green:* Here, sir.
> *Artist:* No. She was called Edith the Fair. They must have been blue.
> *Blue:* Orange! Orange!
> *Orange:* Here, sir.
> *Artist:* As she was in trouble, her cheeks ought to be pale – almost white.
> *White:* Purple and Cherry.
> *Purple and Cherry* (together): Here, sir.
> *Artist:* All the colours –
> *All:* Here we are!
> *Artist:* – of the rainbow, and thanks to the delicacy of my pencil –
> *All:* Brush! brush! (etc., etc.)

The game should be played at a good pace. Forfeits are exacted for mistakes or the slightest hesitations.

What's the Price of Barley? This is yet another of The Mousetrap family. The conductor of the game is called the Master and he gives to the players any names he likes, consisting of simple words, such as:

Player No. 1: Jack
,, ,, 2: How much?
,, ,, 3: What?
,, ,, 4: Too much!
,, ,, 5: Hooray
,, ,, 6: Fifty Shillings
,, ,, 7: Half-a-crown
,, ,, 8: Eighteen pence
,, ,, 9: Good
,, ,, 10: Nonsense

The game is carried on in dialogue, starting with the master, in the following manner:

Master: Jack!
No. 1: Yes, Master.
Master: What's the price of barley?
No. 1: Fifty shillings.
(No. 6 must *not* respond here, his name not having been called by the Master. If he does, and he probably will, he pays a forfeit.)
Master: Good!
No. 9: Yes, Master.
Master: What's the price of barley?
No. 9: Eighteen pence.
Master: Eighteen pence! Nonsense!
8 & 10: Yes, Master.
Master: How much?
No. 2: Yes, Master.
Master: What's the price of barley?
No. 2: Half-a-crown.
Master: Half-a-crown! Hooray! Jack!
7, 5 & 1: (together): Yes, Master.
Master: What's the price of barley?
7, 5 & 1: Half-a-crown, fifty shillings, eighteen pence (or as they feel inclined).
Master: Nonsense!
No. 10: Yes, Master. (Etc., etc.)

Played briskly, this game never fails to produce a splendid collection of forfeits.

The Horned Ambassador: Apart from a few strips of paper all

32

that is required to play this game is a prodigious memory on the part of every player. The strips of paper having been prepared so that they can be attached to the heads of the players, curl-paper fashion, the game begins.

The leader of the game starts by addressing the player seated on his left according to a particular formula which all the other players must repeat after him word for word, without alteration or addition, on pain of receiving the title of Horned Ambassador, instead of that of Royal Ambassador, which all hold at the start of the game. The speech is as follows: 'Good morning, Royal Ambassador, always Royal. I, the Royal Ambassador, always Royal, come from his Royal Majesty, always Royal (indicating the player on his right) to tell you his eagle has a golden beak.'

The second and following players repeat this speech and if anyone makes a mistake, he receives a paper horn in his hair as a punishment for each blunder. In the following round, such a player instead of saying 'I, the Royal Ambassador, always Royal' must say, 'I, the one (or two or three, according to how many horns he has earned) Horned Ambassador, always Horned etc.' By the same rule, when addressing the wearer of one or more horns, it is necessary to say 'Good morning, one (or more) Horned Ambassador, always horned.'

At the second round, the leader adds, and the others repeat successively, a new quality possessed by the king's eagle, such as brazen claws; at the third round, yet another such as diamond eyes; then silver plumes; then iron heart until the round arrives when no one can remember all the splendours of this fabulous bird. Forfeits are then awarded in proportion to the number of horns that have been distributed.

My Lady's Toilet: All the players adopt the name of the various articles connected with the mystery of a Victorian Lady's Toilet, such as Buckles, Bouquet, Fan, Gloves, Necklace, Bracelet, Brooch, etc. The game then proceeds in exactly the same way as in Spinning the Trencher (*see* p. 43), except that the spinner says 'My lady is going to dress for a ball and wants —— (her *gloves*, her *ear-rings* or any other article agreed upon). As he pronounces the word, the spinner gives the trencher its twist and the player called upon darts from his seat (which is taken by the spinner) and tries to catch the trencher before it falls to the ground. Forfeits reward failures. The spinner may occasionally vary the proceedings by, instead of naming a particular article, making use of the word *toilet*. At this signal all players change places, the speaker rushing for the nearest chair. Anyone found after the scuffle in the same place as before pays a forfeit, as must also the player who is left without a seat at all; the latter takes the next spin of the trencher. The spinner may also use the word *twilight*, as, for instance, by saying: 'My lady is going out this evening at . . . *twilight*.' At this no one is allowed to move on pain of forfeit. The similarity of the two words usually leads to a general mêlée.

This Is My Eye: One player starts the game by touching his eye and saying that it is something else. The next player (who must be called by name) touches the part named and calls it something else.

> *1st Player* (touching his eye): This is my thumb, George.
> *George* (touching thumb): This is my chin, Jill.
> *Jill* (touching chin): This is my nose, Anthony.
> *Anthony* (touching nose): This is my ear, Sally.
> *Sally* (touching ear): This is my ear, Mark.
> MISTAKE – Sally is out.

Many mistakes are made if the game is played rapidly. Two mistakes are allowed each player and the last one in is the winner.

Family Snap: This is a energetic version of the ordinary game of Snap, played without cards and with a goodly number of young children.

A list of imaginary names is made out, the number being about twice that of the number of players. The names should be of a comical nature. Also, they should bear a confusing similarity one to the other: Sir Jasper Hogwash, Professor Pinhead, Lady Tartan McClan, Lord Clan McTartan, Sir Jasper Pinhead, Lady

Tartan McHogwash etc. Each of the participants is then allotted a name from this list and this is recorded on a card. These names, together with the unallotted names, are then called out by the referee of the game, one every few seconds and the players have to 'snap' when they hear the name of an actual participant. Points are scored as follows.

Snapping the name of another player.........3 points
Snapping one's own name....................1 point
Snapping an unallotted name *LOSES* ....2 points

With a large and lively party it is advisable for the referee to have an assistant watching out for and checking the 'snaps'.

Russian Gossip: This is a game from which more than one lesson can be learned – the more so if there are a good many players. First of all a circle is formed. Then one player whispers into the ear of his neighbour some little incident, real or imaginary, an anecdote or a piece of gossip. The receiver of the news then whispers it to the next player and so on, around the circle, until it returns to its source. It is then repeated aloud and compared with its original to which it will often bear no resemblance whatsoever.

Buzz: This game requires all a player's wits, otherwise he will find himself out very early in the proceedings. The first player says 'one', the next 'two', the next 'three' and so on until seven is reached. Instead of saying 'seven' the player whose turn it is must say, 'Buzz'. At every multiple of seven – 14, 21, 28, 35, 42 etc. – the word 'Buzz' must be substituted as it must in every number containing a seven – 17, 27, 37, etc. At 77, the player should say, 'Buzz-buzz'. Any player who fails to 'Buzz' is out of the game, the last player being the winner.

Another Form of Buzz: In this version of the game the multiples of seven (i.e. 14, 21, 28 etc.) are left unchanged, only the numbers actually containing the figure seven being replaced by 'Buzz'. The added complication is that after the number 17 (which is 'Buzz') has been passed the sevens are replaced in this manner: 26, 20-Buzz, 28 etc. Then, 36, 30-Buzz etc. Seventy is a simple 'Buzz' but from thence the counting is continued 'Buzz-one, Buzz-two etc.' It is surprising how often mistakes are made by missing 'Buzz-buzz' (77) or by giving 'Buzz-ten' instead of 80.

Prophecies: All that is required for this little frolic is a certain amount of tact on the part of the players. The game is only effective when the members of the company are fairly well acquainted. Early on in the proceedings all write down, privately, on pieces of paper, a prediction concerning some other member of the party – that is, something he or she will do or say during the course of the evening. Before the party breaks up, the prophecies are read aloud to be refuted or confirmed – usually the latter.

h. ACTION AND MOVEMENT GAMES

The Trades: A very old game and a very good one. Each player except one selects a trade which he carries on in dumb show, as follows:

> The Tailor stitches a coat.
> The Cobbler mends a shoe.
> The Laundress washes a tub of linen.
> The Painter paints a portrait.
> The Blacksmith hammers at his anvil, etc. etc.

The remaining player is the King of All Trades and he starts the game by exercising whatever trade he pleases (except one already chosen by another player). In doing this he sets an example of industry to all the others who must then work away at their own various callings. Now, the King of All Trades is also a master of all trades so he can, whenever it pleases him, change his trade and adopt that of another of the party. When this happens, all leave off work at once, except the player thus imitated, who immediately takes up the trade the King has just left off and continues to exercise it until such time as His Majesty decides to change again and to take up the work of yet another player. This worker then takes up the King's trade and continues until another change is made, the other players remaining idle until the King resumes his original occupation which is a signal for all to get back to work. Mistakes earn forfeits.

I Went to Paris: The first player remarks to the second player, 'I went to Paris'. The second player asks, 'What did you buy there?' and the first player replies, 'A pair of shoes' at the same time moving his feet as if he were walking; this movement must be continued throughout the game. The second player then says to the third, 'I went to Paris' and is asked what he bought there. He also bought a pair of shoes and moves *his* feet in the same manner as player number one. This is repeated right around the circle until all the players are moving their feet. At this point the first player again says 'I went to Paris' and upon being asked what he bought says 'A fan' (or any other article that may enter his head) and goes through the motions of fanning himself (while still continuing the movement of his feet). The game continues until all the players have bought, for instance, gloves (finger-wiggling), spectacles (eye winking), cake (munching movement). When the game has reached this point the players are stamping their feet, opening and closing their mouths, fanning themselves with one hand, wiggling the fingers of the other and winking their eyes. Forfeits as usual.

The Promenade Concert or *The Dutch Concert:* The author of *Round Games* tells us that:

This is a nice quiet game. It is solely on that account that we like it. The players seat themselves in a circle, after the fashion of the band in Kensington Gardens – each adopting a musical instrument, on which he is supposed to be the performer. As, for instance, one chooses the violin and draws his right hand backwards and forwards with a vigorous action, expressive of that liberal measure known in musical circles as 'plenty of bow', over his extended left arm; another, the cornet – and puffs out his cheeks to the utmost extent of endurance, and with an entire disregard of personal beauty; another the clarionet – and turns his eyes inside out, prolonging his count-enance as painfully as possible; another the double drum – and knocks as much dust out of two music-stools as possible; another the piano – and strums with his hands on his knees or a table: and so on, through as many instruments as there are performers – the more absurd and ill-suited to an orchestra the better – as the banjo, the Jew's-harp, comb and paper, etc. Triangles, cymbals, tambourines and the noisiest instruments, generally are recommended in preference to those of a more tame and peaceful character. As a rule, however, the most delightful harmony will be found to proceed from the greatest possible variety. Each player must imitate the action, and, as closely as possible, the sound peculiar to his adopted instru-ment – selecting any tune he may think best calculated to display his powers. No two players can, on any account, be allowed to play the same tune; and the greatest enthusiasm must be thrown into the performance. Gravity is indispensable (because next to impossible) and the slightest infraction of it costs a forfeit. The conductor takes his place in the centre of the circle, sitting cross-legged on a chair, with his face to the

back of it, on which he beats time. When the 'Row Polka' is at
its height, and has reached a pitch of Bedlamite confusion, the
conductor suddenly singles out one of the performers and asks
him why he is at fault. The individual thus unexpectedly
pounced upon, must immediately give some excuse for his
want of accuracy, which excuse must be in keeping with the
nature of his instrument. For instance the fiddler replies, that
his 'bridge is broken, and it must be mended'; the harper that
he has broken a string; the pianist, that he has left one of the
keys of his instrument at home on his dressing table; etc. etc.
Any delay in this, or repetition of an excuse already given,
costs a forfeit.

Flying: The company seat themselves each with his right hand
placed on his left arm. The game-leader sits in front and tells a
story that includes as many animals as possible (he may, if he
prefers, merely recite a list of animals). The point of the game is
that every time a flying creature is mentioned each right hand
must be raised and fluttered in the air in imitation of flying.

This once very popular party game is not quite as simple as
might first appear. Many birds – the ostrich, penguin and emu,
for instance – cannot fly, while bats, which are not birds, do fly.
Some insects fly, others do not and if the game is played fairly
rapidly many forfeits will be taken.

38

Fishermen: This centuries-old game was introduced to the English parlour from Russia at about the turn of the last century. Each player fastens to his back a piece of heavy thread but light enough to snap off if stepped upon. It should be just long enough to trail on the floor and on the loose end will be fastened some small object, such as a cotton reel or pencil or anything heavy enough to trail. On the signal to begin, each player tries to step on the other players' 'fish', so as to snap the thread and allow the first player to take it up. At the same time he tries to save his own fish from being caught. No player must touch any fish-line (and this includes his own) with his hands. As each player loses his fish he retires from the game and the catcher of most fish is the winner.

Feather: A small, fluffy feather is required to play this game. The players draw their chairs in a circle as closely as possible. One of the party throws the feather into the air as high as possible. He then blows upon it to keep it floating in the air. The player to whom it comes nearest does the same, in order to prevent it touching him – an accident which demands from him a forfeit. One of the joys of this game is the spectacle of the players trying to blow whilst laughing – a quite impossible operation. This very simple game is recommended as a great producer of both merriment and forfeits.

Potato Race: A number of potatoes and as many spoons and baskets (or other receptacles) are required. The baskets are arranged about a yard apart on one side of the room and from each basket a number of potatoes are placed at intervals of a foot or so to the opposite end. Each player is given a spoon and his task is to spoon up all the potatoes on his line and put them into his basket. The potatoes must be picked up and carried with the spoon alone and must not be touched by any part of the body. If a potato is dropped *en route* to its basket it must be picked up (with the spoon) carried back to its starting place put back on the floor and the player must recommence. The first player to get all his potatoes into his basket is the winner.

Hot Cockles: One player kneels down hiding his eyes by laying his head on a chair. He puts one hand behind him, palm uppermost which the other players strike with their hands. The simple point of this game is for the kneeling player to guess who strikes him. When he is successful the striker takes his place. This game was noticed by John Gay:

> As at hot-cockles once I laid me down,
> I felt the weighty hand of many a clown;
> Buxoma gave a gentle tap, and I
> Quick rose and read soft mischief in her eye.

Putting the Tail on the Donkey: This most unsophisticated of all parlour games still causes much merriment. The necessary equipment – a tailless donkey together with his missing appendage – can be purchased yet. The pin used to affix the tail has now been replaced by a magnetic device (of course) thus making a game which need cost no more than a few pence an elaborate and more expensive one. However, it requires very little talent to draw the outline of a donkey on a piece of paper making it about 18 inches long from its nose to where the tail should be and to cut out the tail which will be put into place by means of a drawing pin. Each player stands about six feet from the donkey, is given the tail and blindfolded. The purpose of the game is obvious.

Another method of play is to have a number of tails, all marked with a number. As each tail is positioned it is left in place while the next player takes his turn. When all have made their attempt, the player who pinned his tail nearest to its correct position is the winner.

Blowing Out the Candle: This is a similar game to pinning the tail on the donkey. A candle is placed on a table and each player in turn is placed a few feet away from it and blindfolded. His task is to advance towards the candle and to blow it out within the space of time that it takes the rest of the company to count to twenty in unison. The attempts of the blindfolded one cause much laughter which infects him and makes his attempts to purse his lips for blowing ludicrous in the extreme. Failure to extinguish the candle means a forfeit and it is only the player with an iron-disciplined mind and an unerring sense of direction who gets through the game unscathed.

The Cushion Dance: A cushion is placed in the middle of the room around which the players form a circle with joined hands, having previously arranged themselves into two sides. They circle the cushion a few times and then one side tries to pull the other side forward so as to force one of their number to touch the cushion with his foot. The ensuing struggle is usually fairly intense and ultimately someone's foot touches the cushion and that person has to leave the circle. When one side has been completely eliminated the other side is proclaimed as the winner.

O'Grady Says: This game invariably results in a rich crop of forfeits. One of the players takes command under the name of 'O'Grady' and everything O'Grady says must be obeyed or a forfeit given. It must be remembered that every order to be obeyed must be preceded with the words 'O'Grady says.' The game proceeds as follows: 'O'Grady says do this' (raising a hand, for example). The players follow suit; then 'O'Grady says do this' (he does something else). Then 'Do this!' This command must be ignored on pain of forfeit.

The Rule of Contrary: In playing this game the word 'contrary' has always been pronounced 'contrairy'. This is because the game, which originated in Cornwall in the eighteenth century or earlier, used to start with the players reciting the following lines:

> Here I go round the rules of contrary
> Hopping about like a little canary
> When I say, 'Hold fast', leave go;
> When I say, 'Leave go', hold fast.

The verse has changed but 'contrary' still has to rhyme with 'canary'. Such is the conservatism of children.

The rules of the game are simple. All the players, standing up, take hold of a large square scarf. One player, taking hold with the rest, starts the game by saying:

> Here we go by the rule of contrary;
> When I say, 'Hold fast', let go;
> When I say, 'Let go', hold fast.

He then says 'Let go' or 'Hold fast' as he chooses. When he says 'Let go', all those who do so pay forfeit; when he says 'Hold fast', all who do not let go are similarly punished. It may be thought that few fall victim to such a simple contrivance but the game usually produces its fair share of the party's forfeits.

Opposites: The guests are arranged in a semi-circle each with a chair behind him. One of them moves from person to person either performing some action or giving some instruction. The person concerned must do the exact opposite. If told to raise his right leg he raises his left; to take off his hat, he must put it on. One by one the players will drop out and the one that holds out the longest is the winner.

Who's the Leader? All the players stand in a circle except one who is sent out of the room. A leader is appointed whose duty it is to lead the other players in clapping, foot-tapping, knee-bending or any other movement that may occur to him. The players engage in the first movement, say, clapping, and the absent player is recalled. It is his task to discover who is leading the players in their actions. When he thinks the moment is opportune, the leader changes the action from clapping to, say, twiddling his thumbs and the rest of the players follow suit. The players should, of course, keep their eyes off the leader as far as possible. It is surprising how quickly the new movement spreads and how difficult it is to discover the leader. When he *is* discovered, the leader is sent out and a new one is selected. This game improves if the actions are done in time to music. There are no forfeits involved and nobody wins or loses.

Sardines: Like Hide and Seek, Sardines is played in the dark and in as many rooms as possible. One player goes away and hides and the rest spread out to look for him. The hiding place chosen should preferably have a reasonable amount of room. The first seeker to find the hider joins him in the same place, both remaining as quiet as possible. The next successful seeker joins them, again as noiselessly as possible and so on. The game ends when all the sardines but one are wedged into the broom-cupboard or whatever and the last to discover the hiding-place pays a forfeit.

Spinning the Trencher: This game is found in all the earliest parlour game books and was evidently very popular. It is simple enough. All the players sit around the room making as large a circle as possible. The player who starts holds a wooden bread board, or circular tray, which is the 'trencher' and, standing in the middle of the circle, spins it on its side while at the same time calling out the name of another player. The named player must spring up and catch the trencher before it ceases to spin. Failure to do this involves a forfeit. It often happens that the wrong person jumps up and bumps into another. This happens when the spinner looks hard at one person and calls the name of another. (*See* also *My Lady's Toilet*, p. 34.)

Moving Statues: In this game all but two players leave the room and between them form a statue group which remains quite motionless. One player is then called in and makes suggestions for 'improving' the statue. His suggestions will undoubtedly be absurd. When he has done this he is compelled to himself take the most ludicrous position in the group, the player who is now free remaining to see the fun. Another player is then summoned and the process repeated. The game continues thus with an ever-increasing number of spectators inside and an ever-decreasing number of budding sculptors outside.

Nuts in May: This is suitable for young players and is a very pretty game. Two sides are chosen and a line drawn across the middle of the room. The children arrange themselves in two rows, one on either side of the line, facing one another. The game is begun by one row advancing towards the other with joined hands, singing:

> Here we come gathering nuts in May, nuts in May,
> nuts in May,
> Here we come gathering nuts in May, on a cold
> and frosty morning.

They then retreat to their original position, and the opposite side advances, singing in reply:

> Pray, who will you gather for nuts in May, nuts
> in May, nuts in May?
> Pray who will you gather for nuts in May
> on a cold and frosty morning?

The first row then settles upon some player on the opposite side, and again advances, singing:

> We'll gather Edna (or Mary) for nuts in May,
> nuts in May, nuts in May etc.

44

The other side then sings:

> Pray, who will you send to fetch her away, etc.

Then, after deciding who they will send, the first side sings:

> We will send Ernest to fetch her away,
>   fetch her away, fetch her away,
> We will send Ernest to fetch her away, on a
>   cold and frosty morning.

The girl must then stand on one side of the line, and the boy on the other, each trying to pull the other over it. If Ernest wins, Edna will have to join his row; if Edna wins Ernest must join her party. Either way the singing begins again.

Orange and Lemons: Two of the company, one pretending to be an Englishman and the other a Frenchman, stand face to face holding each other's hands to form an arch for the rest to pass through one by one. As the company pass under the bridge the couple forming it sing the famous rhyme.

> Oranges and Lemons,
> Sang the bells of St Clements.
> You owe me five farthings,
> Sang the bells of St Martin's.
> When will you pay me?
> Sang the bells of Old Bailey.
> When I grow rich,
> Sang the bells of Shoreditch.
> When will that be?
> Sang the bells of Stepney.
> That I don't know,
> Sang the great bell of Bow.
> Gay go up and gay go down,
> To ring the bells of London Town.

Then, accelerating their tempo the bridge-makers chant:

> Here comes a candle to light you to bed,
> And here comes a chopper to chop off your head.

At which they bring down their hands to capture a player. The prisoner is asked whether he is English or French and has to whisper his choice to his captors who then place him on either the French or the English side – these sides being known only to the bridge builders. When all the players have been captured and allocated to one or other of the armies the latter form two waist-held lines and vie with each other as to which is the strongest army, the contest being that the side that pulls its opponents across a given line wins the game.

Jack's Alive: A twist of paper is set alight and the flame blown out to leave a burning ember. This paper is then handed from player to player each saying, as they present it,

> 'Jack's alive, and likely to live,
> If he dies in your hand, you've a forfeit to give.'

(If preferred only the words 'Jack's Alive' may be used.) The player in whose hand the spark expires duly pays a forfeit, for which reason, when Jack is looking tolerably healthy the players are in no hurry to pass him round but take their time in making the pronouncement. As he grows weaker, however, his circulation becomes very rapid indeed as does the spoken formula.

Snapdragon: This is a very old game and was still popular in the 1930s. A quantity of stoned raisins are placed in a bowl and covered with sufficient brandy to soak them thoroughly. The bowl is placed in the centre of the room, the lights put out and the brandy set alight. (The dish should be on a small table covered with newspaper or oilcloth.) The point of the game is, believe it or not, for the children to snatch the flaming raisins (or snap-dragons) from the dish. Flames made by burning brandy have very little heat in them and only a very clumsy player could sustain the slightest burn, while quickness and dexterity will be rewarded with a great many snapdragons. The most likely reason for this pastime's loss in popularity cannot be fear of the N.S.P.C.C. but the fact that brandy can no longer be obtained at eighteen shillings the dozen bottles.

Battledore and Shuttlecock: Battledores, which resemble small tennis racquets, can still be bought, or table-tennis bats can be used as a substitute. The object of the game is simply to keep the shuttlecock in the air for as long as possible – either solo or between a number of players. A balloon makes a good substitute for the shuttlecock.

Drawing-room Tennis with Japanese Fans and Air Balloons.

i. ACTING GAMES

Charades: This, the most famous of all parlour games, was already established as a favourite pastime in the eighteenth century. In a letter written in 1776 Mrs Boscawen wrote, 'Pray, send me some charrades, but I shall not guess them as you do.' The origin of the word is doubtful but it is likely that it derives either from the Provençal *charrà,* to chatter, or from the Spanish *charrada,* the speech or action of a clown.

All that is required to act a charade are a few pieces of clothing, maybe an odd item of furniture or two and various 'props' that can be adapted from ordinary household odds and ends. All else that is needed is a few bright people, not unduly introverted, who will act out the plays. The actors decide on the word to be acted. It must have two or more syllables, each of which has a meaning of its own – 'nutmeg' or 'waterfall', for example. If the latter word is chosen for instance, three little plays are improvised: the first containing the word 'water', the second 'fall' and the last containing the complete word, 'waterfall'. The object of the game is for the members of the audience to guess the word.

The following are a few of the words suitable for charade acting: arrowroot, artichoke, bookworm, brimstone, cowslip, cupboard, cutlet, daybreak, dovetail, earshot, farewell, footman, grandchild, handsome, hardship, helpless, indulgent, inmate, intent, joyful, kindred, lawful, lifelike, loophole, milkmaid, mistake, misunderstand, necklace, nightmare, nutmeg, orphanage, outside, padlock, painful, pilgrim, quicklime, quicksand, ragamuffin, ringleader, roundhead, scarlet, season, sofa, starling, statement, sweetmeat, sweetheart, tendon, threshhold, toadstool, triplet, upright, uproar, vampire, vanguard, waistcoat, waterfall, wedlock, wilful, workmanship, youthful and, for good measure, zealot and zestful (though not, by the way, words like zoological which instantly betray themselves).

For three or more word charades we suggest the following:

artificial	Art-I-Fish-All
persuaded	Purse-Wade-Ed
understandable	Under-Stand-Able
perspicacity	Purse-Pick-A-City
seasonable	Sea-Son-Able
culmination	Cull-My-Nation
intrusive	In-True-Sieve

Tableaux Vivants: Neither speaking, acting nor miming talents are required for this old pastime. The party divides into two or more groups of three or four persons. Each group is left alone in the room for a while during which time its members decide on a scene – historical, biblical, literary etc. – which they then represent as a tableau. The other players are then called in to guess the scene.

In the days when this game enjoyed great popularity, classical scenes and those borrowed from Shakespeare were the favourites. The author of Cassell's *Book of Sports and Pastimes* (1881), tells us that the prettiest Tableaux Vivants (sic) he ever saw was taken from *Winter's Tale*. The tableau he describes would certainly baffle many today. Subjects chosen for Tableaux Vivants might represent a dramatic moment from some television programme or some popular contemporary personality. Here are a few alternative suggestions:

> Florence Nightingale (lamp and wounded soldiers)
> Sir Francis Drake and Queen Elizabeth (cloak etc.)
> The three witches from *Macbeth*
> King Canute
> Romeo and Juliet (balcony scene)
> Snow White and the Seven Dwarfs
> The Sleeping Beauty
> Three Wise Men with the child Jesus.

Acting Proverbs: This simple guessing game is suitable for small parties. Each player in turn fixes upon a proverb and acts it in dumb show before the others, whose task it is to guess the proverb represented. 'Props' may be used. The first player might, for instance, look at a watch or clock, lie down and feign sleep, wake up and consult the watch again and then, after standing up and stretching, throw out his chest to indicate health, count money to show wealth and touch his forehead with his finger to demonstrate wisdom. Other proverbs that can be acted include 'a rolling stone gathers no moss', 'there's many a slip 'twixt cup and lip', etc.

What Am I Doing? This may be regarded as a sort of 'solo charades'. One player stands in front of the rest of the party and goes through the motions of doing something – the more ludicrous the better. Thus he may imitate the formidable task of washing down an elephant; he may pretend to do a jig-saw or catch a flea. The other players must try to guess his occupation and if they are successful in doing so the actor must pay forfeit. This game is sometimes played with two principal actors, in which case they are allowed a minute or two of conspiracy to decide on their pretended task.

j. KISSING GAMES

Postman's Knock: This game can be used as a forfeit or played for its own sake. First of all, someone is stationed at the door *inside* the room to answer the knocks that will be made. Another person, the 'postman', goes outside the room and gives two knocks on the door. When the door is opened the postman is asked for whom he has a letter and how many pennies the addressee must give for it. The recipient of the letter (a member of the opposite sex) must then go outside the room and pay the postman not in pennies but in kisses.

The Box of Secrets: This charming old game, which was very popular in France under the name of *la boîte d'amourette*, is simply a means of collecting forfeits – apart from the kissing that is.

The player who starts the game presents a small box to his neighbour on the right, saying, 'I will sell you my box of secrets; it contains three – whom I love, whom I will kiss, and whom I will send about his (or her) business'. The neighbour, taking the box, must reply, 'I will buy your box of secrets. Whom do you love? Whom will you kiss? Whom will you send about her business?' (We are assuming that in this instance the box-seller is a gentleman.) The first speaker then names, in answer to the question, the lady in the company whom he loves, the one he intends to kiss (why these should not be one and the same we do not know, but they must not be), and the one he intends to send about her business. The person to be kissed must submit to the operation on the spot, while the one sent about her business pays a forfeit. The buyer of the box must then sell it to the neighbour on her right.

Describing the game in the nineteenth century a writer remarks that, 'No notice whatever is taken of the loved one, which we are at a loss to account for, except as a satire upon professions of affection generally. In candour, however, we are compelled to confess that we do not believe anything of the kind was ever intended – which is a pity.'

Frincy-Francy: This game was never played in some parlours as it was considered to lack refinement, although compared with some of the kissing games that were allowed, such as the Rabbit's Kiss Forfeit (*see* page 135), it was a pastime quite suitable for a vicar's tea party. The game was more popular at parties given in country farmhouses and was frequently played between dances.

A chair is placed in the middle of the room; the master of ceremonies leads to the chair a young lady who, sitting down, names the gentleman she wants to kiss her. He approaches her, kisses her and then takes the seat himself. He then calls out the

name of another lady who is led to him by the master of ceremonies to receive her kiss. This lady then takes the seat, and so
on until everyone has been well kissed. No sex equality here, be
it noted: the gentlemen make their own way to the chair and its
occupant, the ladies must be led!

The Drill Sergeant: The player chosen to be the Drill Sergeant
selects any lady he chooses from the company and conducts her
to the centre of the room. Here he positions himself facing his
troops who have fallen-in in front of him with his lady standing a
few inches behind him, also facing the troops. Like the Sergeant,
each soldier has a lady just behind him. The Sergeant now proceeds to drill the troops and in a stern voice gives the following
words of command: 'Attention!' – 'Take ladies' hands!' – 'Right
about face!' – 'Arms round waist!' – 'Make ready!' – 'Present!' –
'Fire!' The last order is, of course, thoroughly understood even
by the uninitiated and each lady receives her amorous salute. In
describing this game in 1854 a writer remarked that, 'In the
present unsettled state of Europe, and with the defenceless state
of our coasts, exercises of this description are laudable, as
calculated to encourage a martial and patriotic spirit.'

k. ROMP GAMES

Obstacle Race: Those who do not know the game are sent out of
the room and brought back one by one. As each player enters, he
is shown a number of obstacles placed in a line on the floor – an
ornament or two, a footstool, a pile of books etc. He is then blindfolded and told to walk over the obstacles without touching them
but before he starts his journey the objects are quietly removed
so that he walks carefully and highsteppingly to avoid what is no
longer there.

Change: The players form a circle standing close together and
each is given an article to hold. All the articles must be different
and of varying size and weight. A possible list is as follows:

    A walnut
    A book
    A cushion
    A bucket half-full of water
    A frying pan
    An ash tray
    A carpet sweeper

A suitcase
A feather

On the word 'Go' each player passes his object to the player on his right who passes it on to the player on *his* right, this continuing until the command 'Change' is given by a non-player. At this all the articles are passed in the opposite direction. To complicate the circular transit of the objects two or three of them are designated always to be passed in the opposite direction to the rest. This, together with the necessity of successively handling light objects, heavy objects, large objects and small objects is a great test of muscular co-ordination and is the cause of much confusion. Any player who is detected in passing, or trying to pass, an object in the wrong direction, and any player who drops an object must retire from the circle although the object concerned remains in the game leaving the remaining players with a more difficult task. If all the players are eliminated except three or four they will find themselves with armfuls of household articles of mixed character and the exchanges become very difficult and complicated.

Quakers' Meeting: The company arrange themselves on the floor in a straight line, all kneeling on the right knee while on the other knee they rest their hands and twiddle their thumbs. It is forbidden to smile – any player detected doing so having to pay a forfeit. The following conversation is then carried on, each line of which must be repeated in turn by every player before the next line is said.

Well friend, and how art thou?
Hast thou heard of Brother Obadiah's death?
No, how did he die?
With one finger up (As each player repeats this line
he stops twisting his thumbs and holds up his right
forefinger),
With one eye shut (Each closes his right eye),
And shoulder all awry (Each does this).
How did he die?
In this way.

At this point the player at the top of the row gives his neighbour a mighty shove and the whole company goes over like a pack of cards.

Cutlets: This variation of Quakers' Meeting was immortalized by Charles Pooter in his *Diary of a Nobody* and cannot be better described than in his own words.

. . . as it was cold, we stayed in and played games; Gowing, as usual, overstepping the mark. He suggested we should play 'Cutlets', a game we never heard of. He sat on a chair, and asked Carrie to sit on his lap, an invitation which dear Carrie rightly declined. After some species of wrangling, *I* sat on Gowing's knees and Carrie sat on the edge of mine. Lupin sat on the edge of Carrie's lap, then Cummings on Lupin's, and Mrs Cummings on her husband's. We looked very ridiculous and laughed a good deal. Gowing then said: 'Are you a believer

Gowing said : " So am I," and suddenly got up.

in the Great Mogul?' We had to answer all together: 'Yes – oh, yes!' (three times). Gowing said: 'So am I,' and suddenly got up. The result of this stupid joke was that we all fell on the ground, and poor Carrie banged her head on the corner of the fender.

Rejected Addresses: This is a noisy game and a merry one. All the gentlemen leave the room and the ladies arrange a row of chairs according to the number of men. Each of the absent gentlemen has a chair allocated to him but no indication is given as to which chair belongs to which gentleman. A lady then takes up a place behind each chair, care being taken that no lady stands behind the chair allotted to her particular favourite. The gentlemen are then called in, one by one. As each enters all the ladies invite him to sit on her particular chair, each assuring him that he is the one allotted to it. Each lady will use all her feminine arts, charms and wiles to tempt him into her chair. If the victim should be blandished into sitting in the wrong chair all the ladies swoop upon him, pushing him, shoving him and beating him with cushions until he is forced out of the room again. Should he be fortunate enough to choose the right chair he is allowed to stay in the room and watch the fun.

Hiss and Clap: This is a more subdued version of the preceding game. After all the gentlemen have left the room the ladies take their seats, each leaving a vacant space on their right-hand side for the gentleman of their choice. Each gentleman is summoned in turn and is asked which lady has chosen him for her partner. If he guesses correctly he is clapped by the rest of the company and allowed to take his seat next to the lady who has chosen him; otherwise he is loudly hissed until he leaves the room.

The Knight of the Whistle: This game is only successful if a player can be found who does not know its secret. He is made the hunter. First he has to submit to the ceremony of conferring upon him the Knighthood of the Whistle. During this ceremony the whistle, which is on the end of a piece of string, is surreptitiously attached to the back of the hunter's coat with a bent pin. He is then told to detect the player who has the whistle in his closed hand. None has, for the object of the game is for the other players to blow the whistle behind the hunter's back and, of course, each time he turns around to locate it, it is again blown behind him. It generally takes the knight a considerable time to discover that the object of his search is fastened to himself.

The Jolly Miller: A fairly large and unencumbered space is required to play this game which, by the way, is described in Cassell's *Book of Pastimes* as 'not one of the most refined of occupations'. Each gentleman chooses a lady for a partner except the one who is to be the miller. He, the solitary one, takes his place in the middle of the room while his companions arm in arm in couples walk around him singing the following:

> There was a jolly miller who lived by himself.
> As the wheel went round he made his wealth;
> One hand in the copper and the other in the bag,
> As the wheel went round he made his grab.

At the word 'grab' all the players must change partners while the miller tries to secure a lady for himself; then, needless to say, the unlucky gentleman without a partner takes up the lonely position in the middle of the ring.

The Queen of Sheba: All the gentlemen are sent out of the room. The ladies then select one of their number to play the Queen and the game proceeds thus. The first gentleman is recalled, as though he himself was to undergo the ordeal of 'kissing the Queen of Sheba'. In fact, the secret is explained to him and he joins the fair conspiracy, which is as follows.

All the ladies sit on the floor in two rows, facing each other, their legs extended so that their feet just touch. At the end of this lane and facing the door sits the 'Queen of Sheba' with a veil or shawl over her head. The second gentleman is then brought in and told that if he can pass through the lane of ladies *blindfolded* without stepping on any limb he will be allowed to kiss the Queen. As soon as this player has been blindfolded the Queen gives up her position to the 'King' (the first gentleman to have entered the room) who assumes the throne and the veil and sits awaiting the kiss. Meanwhile, all the ladies have drawn in their feet to leave the path to the Queen unimpeded. Unaware of this, the blindfolded player will perform the most extraordinary acrobatics to reach the Queen and deliver the kiss. He will probably receive some little guidance from the ladies on either side. When he finally delivers the kiss the blindfold is removed to the delighted squeals of the Queen and her Court. To allay the suspicions of the waiting gentlemen after the *first* of their number has been called in, it is a good idea for the ladies to simulate merriment after initiating the first gentleman into the secret of the game.

Feeding the Baby: Two volunteers are blindfolded and sit on the floor with knees touching. Each is given a bowl of broken biscuits, crumbled cake or cornflakes and a wooden spoon. A *wooden* spoon is essential if serious injuries are to be avoided. On the word 'go' each player endeavours to feed the other by filling his spoon and steering it into his partner's mouth. The spectacle is exceedingly funny.

Walking the Plank: A length of tape, about the length of the room, is laid upon the floor and each person present has to walk its length while looking through a pair of binoculars or opera glasses the wrong way round. The contortions, poses and facial expressions that result are quite extraordinary.

Crossing Niagara: A number of players are sent out of the room while the remainder prepare the scene as follows. A plank of wood some six feet long is suspended between two chairs. The first player is brought into the room and informed that he is to be blindfolded and hoisted onto the plank which he must then walk. While he is undergoing the operation of being blindfolded, the plank is quietly taken from the chairs and laid on the floor. The blind man is then hoisted up by two other players and put down on the plank which he will then walk much in the manner of the Great Blondini.

Barnyard: One of the company goes around to the others *supposedly* whispering the name of a farmyard animal to each. In fact, he tells them all to remain silent except one. This player is given 'rooster' and on the command to the company for each person to imitate his animal altogether, all remain silent except for the solitary crowing of the rooster.

Topsy-Turvey Concert: This antic is so ridiculous that it is extremely funny. Some slight preparation is required before the game begins. The performers should be children of about the same height and they should know the words of some catchy popular song which has both verse and chorus. *John Brown's Body* is a good example. A sheet is stretched across the room, so that when the performers are standing behind it only their heads can be seen by the rest of the party who constitute the audience. Before starting the performance, the players place socks or stockings on their arms and shoes on their hands. (This is done in secrecy, behind the sheet.) At a given signal (and preferably with piano-forte accompaniment) they all start singing. During the verse ('John Brown's Body, etc') they keep their hands and arms care-fully hidden behind the sheet, but on the commencement of the chorus ('Glory, Glory Halleluiah') the singers quickly stoop down to hide their heads and thrust up their arms and hands, wildly waving them around to the music, the effect being that of a row of people singing whilst standing on their heads. At the beginning of the second verse the heads appear again but each chorus is sung by the players apparently standing on their heads.

Brother I'm Bobbed: Two chairs are placed side by side in the middle of the room and upon these chairs sit two blindfolded players, each supplied with a rolled-up newspaper. It is essential that one of the players knows the game while the other does not. The player who knows the game removes his blindfold and hits himself on the head with his newspaper saying, 'Brother I'm bobbed!' The other blindfolded player asks, 'Brother, who bobbed you?' and the first player answers, pretending to guess one of the other players in the room. He then hits his neighbour on the head who in his turn says, 'Brother, I'm bobbed.' 'Brother, who bobbed you?' the first player asks. The second player then tries to guess the name of his assailant but never, of course, gets it right. The action is continued until the novelty wears off – a half a dozen bobs apiece is usually sufficient.

He Can Do Little Who Cannot Do This: This very simple game was a great favourite with Victorian children. Only those who know the secret escape paying a forfeit.

The first player (who must be in the know) takes a stick, umbrella or broom in his hand and thumps it three or four times on the floor afterwards saying, 'He can do little who cannot do this.' He then passes the stick to the next player who is supposed to do exactly the same on pain of forfeit. The secret is that the first player thumps the stick with his left hand while subsequent players take it in their right.

Pillow Fight: Two players are blindfolded and given a pillow apiece. They are put into opposite corners of the room and told that a point will be awarded for every blow delivered to the enemy. At this, they advance towards one another but, unknown to either of them, another player, *unblindfolded*, has also been furnished with a pillow and he hits first one then the other of the two blindfolded contestants, who meanwhile beat the empty air with their pillows and score very few points indeed.

Mirror Drawing: Each player is asked to draw an object, say a pig, on paper while looking through a mirror and not directly at the paper. A particularly difficult object to draw is a watch with its hand pointing to a definite time.

2 Word Games

IN THIS category, only those games which require nothing more than the power of speech for their performance are included. Word games requiring any equipment such as a board, diagram or even a pencil are dealt with in the following section (although in the case of Proverbs and The Elements the use of a pocket handkerchief is allowed). The advantages of word games are that they can be played by any number of people without forethought or preparation, at any time and in any place. 'From thence to the Hague,' wrote Pepys, 'again playing at Crambo in the Wagon.'

The majority of the many word games played by the Victorians would probably seem tedious to the modern player. There was, for instance, Decapitations, a game in which every player had to find a word which, when one of its end letters was removed, left another word that could be similarly decapitated and so on

(Abate, bate, ate, at, a). Then there were Anagrams, Word Squares and Enigmas – the latter game played around a chosen subject as, for example, birds: Q. What does a sore throat prevent you from doing? A. Swallow. Q. Who was a famous architect? A. Wren. etc. Paragrams, Extractions, Definitions, Inversions, Metagrams and Chronograms are but a few of the soporifics best omitted.

The author Stephen Leacock was brought up in the period and he well remembered the Jolly Maiden Aunt, whose presence was inevitable at every party, suggesting all the usual word games:

> What is the difference between an elephant and a silk hat? Or declare that her first is a vowel, her second a preposition, and her third an archipelago . . . [and] instructing each player to challenge the player holding the golden letter corresponding to the digit next in order, to name a dead author beginning with **X**, failing which the player must declare himself in fault, and pay the forfeit of handing over to the Jolly Aunt his gold watch and all his money, or having a hot plate put down his neck.

Most of the word games given here will be found suitable for play among mixed age groups and ideal for relieving the tedium of long journeys by road or rail.

Crambo: For some reason this game was the most popular of all Victorian parlour games. No party, adults' or children's, would have been complete without a few rounds of Crambo. The origin of the name of the game is not known.

One player leaves the room while the rest select a word. The guesser is then called in. He or she is told a word that rhymes with the chosen one and must go on to guess, *without naming them*, other words that rhyme with the chosen word until the latter is discovered. For example, let us suppose the chosen word is *play* and the clue given to the guesser is *hay*. The game might then continue as follows:

Guesser:	Is it a month in Spring?
Omnes:	No, it is not May.
G.	Is it a path to somewhere?
O.	No, it is not way.
G.	Is it the opposite to night?
O.	No, it is not day.

And so on until the word is discovered or the company fall asleep.

Another version, known as *Dumb Crambo* is played as follows. Half the company leave the room while the other half decide on

61

a word which *must* be a verb. When the first team return they are
told another verb that rhymes with the one to be guessed.
Suppose the latter is *smell*, the guessing team might be given
propel as the clue and from that clue they must *act* the word they
think to be the correct one. They might, for example, act the
felling of a tree. Then, being wrong, they are hissed by their
opponents. The procedure is continued until the right verb is
discovered and acted.

Grandmother's Trunk: This is one of the oldest word games on
record. Each player has to repeat an ever-increasing list of
objects and to do so without so much as a smile. The first player
starts by saying, 'My Grandmother keeps an anchor in her trunk'
(or any article beginning with the letter A). The player on his left
must think of an article beginning with B, such as 'boot polish'
and say, 'My Grandmother keeps anchors and boot polish in her
trunk'. Thus the game continues, each player having to remember
all the odds and ends kept in his Grandmother's trunk and to try
to add one so ridiculous that it will make one of his fellow-players
smile or laugh. The latter entails disqualification as does an
inability to remember the full list of Grandmother's possessions.

The Traveller's Alphabet: The first player says, 'I am going to
Amsterdam' (or any other place beginning with A). The player
on his left then asks, 'What will you do there?' and must be
answered with a sentence in which the verb, adjective and noun

62

begin with the letter A. The second player now announces his departure for Belgium or any place beginning with a B and is likewise questioned. The game goes like this.

1. I am going to Amsterdam.
2. What will you do there?
1. I shall artfully avoid anchovies.
2. I am going to Belgium.
3. What will you do there?
2. I shall bury bullocks' bones.
3. I am going to Canada.
4. What will you do there?
3. I shall catch a craven coward.

And so on until X, Y and Z are dealt with (Heaven forfend!) or another game is called for. Forfeits for failures and mistakes, of course.

Ship's Alphabet: A Captain is elected and the rest of the players sit in front of him. The Captain points to the first player and asks, 'The name of the letter?' The name of the letter *must* be A and all the questions must be answered with a word beginning with A. The next letter must be B and so forth.

Captain:	The name of the letter?
Player 1:	A
Captain:	The name of the ship?
Player 2:	Alec
Captain:	The name of the captain?
Player 3:	Arthur
Captain:	The name of the cargo?
Player 4:	Apples
Captain:	The port she came from?
Player 5:	Amsterdam
Captain:	The place she is bound for?
Player 6:	Agra
Captain:	The name of the letter?
Player 1:	B etc.

All answers must be given before the captain can count ten and failures or mistakes involve forfeits.

The Minister's Cat: Any number can play this game and the more the merrier. The first player describes the minister's cat with any adjective beginning with the letter A. For instance, 'The minister's cat is an angry cat'. The next player must also use an A. 'The

63

minister's cat is an amiable cat'. This continues for one round, at which the letter B is taken and so on throughout the alphabet. Players drop out if they are unable to find an adjective or if they repeat one already used. The game *can* get past X for see 'xenial', 'Xeresian', or 'xenophobic' as only three examples.

I Love My Love: This very old game can be played by any number of players. The players merely have to answer a number of questions with epithets, all of which must begin with the same letter, as in this example:

> Why do you love your love?
> Because he is amiable.
> Why do you hate your love?
> Because he is argumentative.
> Where did you meet your love?
> At the sign of the Angel.
> What did he feed you there?
> He fed me on asparagus.
> What is the name of your love?
> His name is Archibald.
> Where does your love live?
> He lives at Andover.

When one player has got this far, the questioning passes to the next who has to answer with words beginning with the letter B. The game goes on throughout the alphabet with the exclusion of X and Z. Players are out if they cannot answer a question correctly and at once or if during a second time round they repeat an answer already used.

I Love My Love (a simpler version):
The profession of love is simplified as follows:

> A. I love my love with an A, because he is Affectionate, because his name is Augustus, I will give him an Amethyst, feed him on Apple-tart and make him a bouquet of Anemones.
> B. I love my love with a B, because she is Beautiful, because her name is Beatrice. I will give her a Brooch, feed her on Black-pudding and make her a bouquet of Bluebells.

'Andsome, 'Onorable, 'Orrible or Helegant are not allowed in either versions of this game.

Forbidden Letters: A letter of the alphabet is chosen and the players are forbidden to use it in any word when answering the selected questioner. Furthermore a player must not answer with the words 'yes' or 'no'. If, for example, the forbidden letter is 'E' and the question is 'Do you like this game?', the answer cannot be 'yes', 'no', 'I like it' or any other reply containing an 'e'. His reply *could* be 'Not much' or 'A bit'. If a player answers wrongly he is out.

Flour Merchant: The player taking the part of the flour merchant must try to sell his stock of flour by asking questions of the other players one by one. The others must resist his salesmanship but without using the words 'flour', 'I', 'yes' or 'no'. Any player caught using one of these words must pay a forfeit.

Do you want some flour today?
None is required.
Let me persuade you to take a sample.
Impossible.
Why?
You heard my answer.
Then I must have forgotten it. What was it?
I won't take any.

The flour merchant having succeeded in obtaining an 'I' goes on to the next player.

Proverbs (1): The players sit in a circle. One has a rolled-up hand-kerchief or a ball of paper which he suddenly throws at any other player. The company now count up to ten in unison and before they finish the person hit must quote a proverb. Proverbs must not be repeated and any player who fails to speak in time must retire or pay a forfeit.

Proverbs (2): One of the company is sent out of the room. The rest decide on a proverb, a well-known quotation, or any known expression to be discovered by him on his return. To effect the discovery he is entitled to ask questions from the company all round, beginning with the player on his left. He may ask any question he pleases, but the answer must contain the first word of the proverb, the answer to the second must contain the second word, and so forth, each member of the party taking a word in succession, and the questions going round the company as many times as are necessary until the proverb is completed. The great difficulty in this game is to contrive answers in such a way that the fatal word is not conspicuous. It is best to choose proverbs or quotations composed of the most common words such as 'Many hands make light work', and *not* those that give themselves away like 'Too many cooks spoil the broth'. If, for instance, the chosen proverb was 'Procrastination is the thief of time', the game would not survive the first word.

Shouting Proverbs: As in the previous game, one player leaves the room while the others agree upon a proverb. One word of the proverb is given to each of the company, any players being left over having to stand down for this round of the game. The guesser then returns, stands in front of the other players and orders 'Load! Aim! FIRE!' At the word 'Fire' the party all shout out their particular words together and from the resulting noise he is expected to guess the proverb. He is allowed three attempts.

Quotations: One person, usually the host, quotes half a quotation to the first guest in the line and asks him to complete it. It is best, of course, to write down a number of familiar quotations in preparation for this game. Thus:

> 'All that glitters . . . is not gold'
> 'Give me liberty or . . . give me death'
> 'Come into the garden, Maud . . . For the black bat, night, has flown'

Poet's Chair: The Poet's Chair is set in the middle of the room and the players sit around it. The first Poet takes the chair and recites any line of poetry, or if preferred, a couplet.

> 'You are old Father William' the young man cried
> 'The few locks that are left you are gray.'

The players must now try to think of a line of poetry beginning with the letter G, i.e. the initial letter of the last word of the last quotation. The first to do so claims the Poet's Chair.

> Green grow the Rushes, O.

The next line must begin with an O:

> Onward Christian soldiers.

No line may be used more than once and there is no scoring.

Endless Story: The participants sit in a circle and one of them starts off a story – any story at all. He may continue for up to a minute and then, without finishing the story, he touches the person on his right who must continue the narrative, even from the middle of a sentence. This continues until the chain reaches the person who started it and he must bring it to a successful conclusion – also within a minute.

One Syllable: The company should be seated in a circle, a lady and gentleman alternately. A lady begins by asking a question to the player on her right to which he must reply by one word of one syllable or incur a forfeit for every extra syllable. Played at a party in the nineteenth century, the conversation might have gone as follows:

Lady: Permit me, sir, to ask if you love music?
Gent: Yes. (Then, to the lady on his right).
         Pray, madam, what wood do you think best for making loggerheads?
Lady: Oak. Pray, sir, who is the cleverest man in the world?
Gent: I. What kind of people prosper most in the world?
Lady: Fools. Pray, sir, are you not romantic?
Gent: Yes. But which is handsomest, you or I?
Lady: I. What sort of girl do you think I am?
Gent: Mad. Which do you prefer, champagne or claret?
Lady: Claret. (She pays a forfeit).

I've Been to Market: The company being formed into a circle, one of the players says to his neighbour on the left, 'I've been to market.' The neighbour enquires, 'What have you bought?' The first player may then name any article that comes into his head, provided that he is able, on saying the word, to *touch* an article such as he has named. This may be an article on his own person, such as a coat, a shoe, a pen etc. or something within his reach such as a carpet, a dress, a brooch, a chair etc. Whoever is unable to name an article not previously indicated is punished by paying a forfeit.

The Elements: The players sit round in a circle and one of them throws a screwed-up handkerchief to another calling at the same time 'Earth' (or 'Air' or 'Water') and then counting, quite rapidly, up to ten. The player to whom the handkerchief is thrown must give the name of some animal that lives on earth (if 'air' is called some bird, or if 'water' is called some fish) before the thrower has counted ten. If he fails he pays a forfeit but either way he throws the handkerchief at someone else, and so on.

Proper Names: One player leaves the room while the rest agree on a proper noun. When he comes back he must ask each person in turn a question in an effort to find out the chosen name. The questions are put as in the game of Twenty Questions but the answers must always be formed in this way (as in Crambo): 'No, it is not . . .' or 'Yes, but it's not . . .' The missing word must *always* begin with the same letter as the chosen word and the answer must always be true. Supposing the chosen word is Beethoven then the dialogue might go like this:

Q. Is it a city in England?
A. No, it is not Birmingham.
Q. Is it a man?
A. Yes, but it's not Bunyan.
Q. Is he alive?
A. No, it is not Betjeman.
Q. Is he a musician?
A. Yes, but it's not Bach.
    etc.

Anyone failing to answer correctly is declared 'out'. The questioner wins if he gets the answer within an agreed time limit, or within a given number of questions. Otherwise he pays a forfeit.

Ghosts: Any number of players can play Ghosts. Each is allowed five lives; when he has lost all five he is out of the game. The first player says a letter, the next adds a letter, the next a third letter and so on. The object of the game is to *avoid* completing a word – the player that does so loses a life, as does a player who cannot add a letter that leads to a word.

Player 1: D
Player 2: DE
Player 3: DEC
Player 4: DECO (He must avoid DECK, for this loses him a life.)
Player 5: DECOR (a foreign word, so allowable)
Player 6: DECORO
Player 7: DECOROU
Player 8: DECOROUS (He has no choice and so loses a life.)

If, for example, Player 7 thinks that there is no word beginning

68

with DECORO he may challenge Player 6 and if Player 6 supplies that word, Player 7 loses a life. If Player 6 cannot give the word he loses a life. The next player after the one who loses a life now starts with another letter and the game continues until only one player remains alive.

3 Table Games

ALL THE games described in the previous chapter can, of course, be played across a table – indeed many are better for it. In this section, however, we include games which, whether or not they require special equipment, are more comfortably played over a table than upon the floor.

GAMES NEEDING NO SPECIAL EQUIPMENT: These, in the main, are word games that require a pencil and paper. The most famous of them is the game of Consequences which was already well-established in the sixteenth century. It is described by Ben Jonson in *Cynthia's Revels:*

Why, I imagine a thing done; Hedon thinks who did it; Maria with what it was done; Anaides, where it was done; Argurion, when it was done; Amorphus, for what cause it was done; you, Philantia, what followed upon the doing of it; and this gentleman, who would have done it better.

The game has continued to be popular up to the present century and was a great favourite in the Victorian parlour.

BOARD GAMES: Hundreds of different board games were played in Victorian parlours but as most of them were played with special boards and pieces which no longer exist we have confined our selection to those that can be played on available or easily made-up boards. Chess and backgammon have been excluded as these games have their own special bibliographies.

That board games have been played for thousands of years is evidenced by drawings found on the walls of Egyptian tombs some 5,000 years old. Sets of the Egyptian game of Senet (also known to the ancients as Thirty Squares) have been found intact, for no Egyptian king was buried without a set of this game with which to help while away eternity in the next world. A set of Senet comprised a board, on which were marked three lines of ten squares each, and a number of pawn-like pieces. The method of playing the game is not known but it is probable that it was similar to that of our backgammon. Another game that was very similar to backgammon was the ancient Roman game of *Duodecim scripta* which was played on a board marked with twelve double lines.

Games of the 'draughts' family have been played since pre-historic times and have even found their way into legend, for Athena found the suitors of Penelope seated on cowhides playing a form of draughts. The earliest form of the game was played by two players with five pieces each on a board marked with five lines. The lines were added to over the years until they numbered eleven and later still these lines developed into the board of squares we use today.

A similar game to draughts which developed independently from the European game is the African *Mancala*, a game that is played under different names and with slightly differing rules by Bantu, Nilotes, Hamites and Semites all over the African continent. So involved is the play and so complicated the rules of *Mancala* that it is rare for a European to master the game.

Even the very Victorian game of Ludo (it was patented and commercialized in the 1890s) has an ancient history and, indeed, a very glamorous one for it is a descendant of the Hindu game of *Parcheesi* (Pachis = 25), invented by one of the old Mogul

71

Emperors. He played it on a courtyard paved in the design of a board and used slave girls as pieces.

DOMINO GAMES: The game of Dominoes was invented in Italy at the end of the seventeenth century and was so named from the ebony backing of each 'card' which, it was said, resembled the cloak known as a domino. Of the twelve varieties of Dominoes, the standard or 'block' game and four other forms that were popular in earlier days are included here.

SOLITAIRE: Finally I have included the 'solo' board game of Solitaire because it is now enjoying a deserved revival. A set of Solitaire looks well even in the most modern parlour and, needing no setting up, it is always handy to provide something to do in idle or waiting moments. With its pretty glass pieces and the satisfying clicking as one by one they are removed, the game provides a calming and relaxing entertainment.

a. PENCIL AND PAPER GAMES

Consequences (Verbal): This delightful old game was a parlour favourite until comparatively recently. Any number of players can take part, each one being supplied with a sheet of notepaper and a pencil. Each player writes down on the top of his paper one or more adjectives that can be applied to human beings – fat, happy, brilliant, ugly, ambitious etc.; he then folds the top of the paper in such a way as to conceal what he has written. Each then passes his paper to the player on his left who writes upon it the name of a man – either one of the company or some celebrity. The papers are again folded and passed to the left, the procedure continuing as follows:

3. Who the man met (this must be a woman)
4. Where they met
5. What he gave her
6. What he said to her
7. What she replied
8. What the consequence was
9. What the world said

The papers are then opened and the resulting episodes are read aloud.

There is a longer version of this game in which the sequence is as follows:

Adjective describing a man
The man's name
What he was wearing
What he was doing at the time

met

Adjective describing the lady
The lady's name
What she was wearing
What she was doing
The person she would much rather have met
Where the meeting took place
What he thought
What he said
What she thought
What she said
Where they went
What they did there
The consequence
What the world said

Celebrities: In this game a leader is chosen and all the other players are supplied with pencil and paper. The leader then announces a letter of the alphabet – in this case let us say 'B'. The players then have three minutes in which to write down all the celebrities they can think of whose names begin with B. They may be actors, businessmen, writers, musicians, murderers, statesmen etc. In case of dispute the leader is the final judge as to whether a person is a celebrity. At the end of the three minutes each player reads his list aloud. One point is allowed for every name that does not appear on any other list. If, therefore, the first player announces Beethoven, then all other players cross Beethoven off their lists. The player with the highest score wins. The art of the game is to choose lesser-known celebrities. For instance, Bartok, Bradshaw, Beaumont and Belloc stand a much higher chance of scoring than do Beethoven, Browning, Beecham and Brahms.

Doublets: This puzzle game, invented by Lewis Carroll, was published in *Vanity Fair* in 1879. The rules of the game are simple, the playing of it is not. Two words are taken, each containing the same number of letters and these words are joined by 'links' forming them into phrases or sentences. Thus 'Drive PIG into STY'. The object of the game is to change the word PIG into the

word STY by changing one letter at a time, but through a chain
of real words, thus:

PIG

pit

sit

sat

say

STY

The player who completes the transposition with the least number
of changes wins that round and is awarded with the same number
of points as there are letters in the two key words. In the above
example, six points would be given.

Other examples are:

Prove a ROGUE to be a BEAST

ROGUE

vogue

vague

value

valve

halve

helve

heave

leave

lease

least

BEAST

Try some of the following.

Raise FOUR to FIVE

Make WHEAT into BREAD

Dip PEN into INK

Touch CHIN with NOSE

Change TEARS into SMILE

PITCH TENTS

Cover EYE with LID

Prove PITY to be GOOD

Make EEL into PIE

Evolve MAN from APE

Make FLOUR into BREAD

Get COAL from MINE

Square Words: A word is selected, its length being a matter of
taste, for the longer the word the more difficult the game. Let us

suppose it to be PASTIME. Each player writes this word on a piece of paper downward on one side, upward on the other.

P	E
A	M
S	I
T	T
I	S
M	A
E	P

The players then have to supply letters to form words which begin and end with the letters as they stand. A fixed time is allowed for this, say five minutes, and at the end of this time each player calls out his words. The words should be as unusual as possible since a word formed by more than one player does not score. Words of less than four letters are not allowed.

The longer the word chosen, the more difficult becomes the game, for in a long word there is more chance of the vowels falling together and the combinations of such vowels as A and U or their reverse are difficult to fit into a word especially if proper nouns are ruled out.

A possible solution to the square given above might be:

P a s t E
A l a r M
S p a g h e t t I
T a i n T
I l l n e s S
Me m o r a n d A
E n w r a P

Gallows or *Hangman:* This ever-popular game can be enjoyed by any number of persons irrespective of age. One player, the hangman, having chosen a word (any word) announces how many letters it contains and marks on a piece of paper the same number of 'blanks'. Suppose the word to be 'Capricorn' (nine letters) the nine blanks are indicated thus: – – – – – – – – –. The condemned man (or men), desperately seeking reprieve, asks the hangman whether the word contains any Es. The answer, in this case, is 'no' and the hangman starts to build his gallows. On next being asked, for example, if there are any Cs, the hangman is compelled to place the Cs on the first and sixth blanks, where they belong and he must postpone the erection of his gallows. The game continues in this manner until the condemned man either wins a reprieve by discovering the word before the gallows is built and the hanging takes place or, until the execution is carried out. The sequence of gallows construction and the 'turning off' is effected as follows.

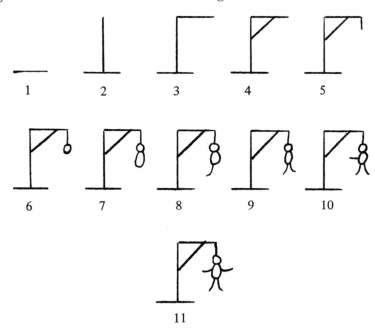

It will be appreciated that more often than not the longer the word, the easier it will be for the condemned to obtain a reprieve; and that even a simple word like 'wry' will usually cost a man his neck. Obscure words are not barred although technical ones usually are. The game is sometimes played by reducing the number of guesses to eight. This is done by omitting the horizontal line on which the gallows stands and assuming that the condemned man has no arms.

Proverbs Gallows: This is played in exactly the same way as Gallows except that a proverb or well-known phrase is used instead of a single word. Taking as an example the phrase 'Hanged by the neck' the letter spaces are laid out as follows:

Generally speaking, a 'proverbs' gallows claims fewer victims than does the ordinary variety.

Guggenheim: Select any word, preferably one with five or six letters none of which are the same. If the word is for instance **OLYMPIA**, it is written down as in the diagram below on as many pieces of paper as there are players – or each player can prepare his own diagram from the dictation of the president. Then, again as below, a list of various categories is made, the number of which is discretionary.

	O	L	Y	M	P	I	A
TOWN	Oslo	London	York	**Macon**	Paris	Ipswich	Andover
BOOK	Oliver Twist	Little Women	Yellow-plush papers	Masterman Ready	Pickwick Papers	I am a Camera	A Tale of Two Cities
RIVER	Oise	Loire	**Yangtze**	Mississippi	Po	Isla	Amstel
POET	Ovid	Longfellow	Yeats	Masefield	T.S. Peacock	Jean Ingelow	Arnold
FLOWER	Oleander	Lily	Yarrow	Marigold	Pansy	Iris	Aster
SHAKESPEARE CHARACTER	Othello	Lear	Young Cato	Macbeth	**Portia**	Iago	Antonio

All the players must now fill up the squares. Each must think of a town beginning with 'O', another beginning with 'L' and so forth. Then the same is done with the books, the rivers and the poets. Depending on what is arranged beforehand the winner may be:

The one who completes his diagram first.

The one who has filled in the most squares within an agreed time.

The one who has the most points based on the following system: if there are ten people playing and they all get Yeats for a poet beginning with 'Y' then they all score one point; if, however, only one player gets Yeats then he scores ten points. In this way the players will strive to think of odd names rather than those that are obvious.

Squares or *Boxes:* A development of noughts and crosses, Squares may be played by two, three or four players. Lines of dots are set out as in the diagram, the size of the square depending upon the length of time desired to play the game.

```
.   .   .   .   .   .
.   .   .   .   .   .
.   .   .   .   .   .
.   .   .   .   .   .
.   .   .   .   .   .
.   .   .   .   .   .
```

77

It will be seen that the large square contains a number of potential small squares that can be made by joining the dots together horizontally or vertically. The players take it in turns to make these joins with the object of obtaining as many of these squares as possible, the square going to the player who adds the completing stroke. The game opens by a selected player drawing a stroke from one dot to another. Each does this in turn, endeavouring to place his stroke in a way that will make it impossible for the next player to complete a square. At first this is simple enough but there comes a point in the game when a player has no choice but to put in the third stroke to a square and leave it for his successor to complete. The player finishing a square writes his initials within it to prove ownership and is allowed another stroke. It will be seen that in completing the first square the player may well open up the opportunity of completing another – and yet another. It is therefore necessary for the previous player to think very carefully in order to keep down that number.

Original Sketches: Each player is supplied with a pencil and paper at the top of which a small sketch is drawn by everyone. The sketch may represent some historical incident, a proverb or any other subject chosen. When all the sketches are completed each player passes his picture to his lefthand neighbour who examines the picture and writes on the *bottom* of the paper what he thinks its meaning to be. He then folds the paper so as to conceal the writing and passes it to the player on *his* left. He, in turn, writes down his interpretation but without looking at what has already been written. As soon as the sketches have been examined and commented on by all the players, they are collected, the papers unfolded and the various opinions read aloud.

The Maze: This is a game for 2 players. A number of dots or small circles are marked out in the form of a square. The first player marks two of the dots and his opponent has to connect them with a line – it need not be the most direct one. The second player then marks two dots and the first player must connect them. The game is easy enough at the beginning but becomes increasingly complex because neither player must touch any unmarked dot or cross or touch upon any line. Each time a player does so he loses a mark.

Up Jenkins: Another very old game. Two sides, each with a captain, seat themselves on either side of a long table. One team possesses a small coin which they pass from hand to hand under cover of the table. Directly he thinks that sufficient time has been given to hide the coin, the captain of the other side calls 'Up Jenkins' and all the closed fists of the coin-holding side are held above the table. The captain then calls 'Down Jenkins' at which the hands are brought down upon the table palms downward. This movement is made as loudly as possible so as to drown the chink of the coin as it strikes the table. The coinless side then put their heads together to try to decide whose hand the coin is *not* under, asking each of the opposing team in turn to show their hands. A clever side will be able to guess with some success by studying the faces and demeanor of the members of the opposing party. Should a mistake be made and a hand called up under which the coin *was* hidden, the coin remains with the same side for the next round. If the last hand left on the counter covers the coin it passes to the guessing side. The side that first scores ten points wins the game.

b. BOARD GAMES

Draughts: This game is for two players and is played on a board of 64 squares, 32 black and 32 white. The board is placed so that each player has a black square at his right-hand lower corner. There are 24 draughtsmen, 12 of each colour. The men are laid out on the white squares of the first three rows on each side of the board. The pieces move diagonally from square to square either to the left or right. They may never move across or straight back or forward. Each player moves forward one square at a time, in turn. Players draw for colour and black starts. The pieces can take by passing over the opposing man into a vacant square – the man taken is removed from the board. Any number of men can be taken in this way in a move. As soon as a man arrives at any of the four squares in the last opposite row, he is crowned and becomes a king (another man is placed on top of the advanced piece). The king has the privilege of moving either backward or forward, but only one square at a time. The object of the game is to capture the enemy's men, or to so block them in that they cannot move; the player who first accomplishes either of these objects wins.

Fox and Geese: This is a game for two players using a draughts-board and five draughtsmen – four white and one black. It is an exciting game requiring some skill but with the drawback that if the player manipulating the four geese (the white pieces) knows the secret, the fox (played by the black piece) cannot possibly elude them.

The object of the game is for the geese to force the fox into a corner while the fox tries to elude them and get through to the opposite side of the board. The geese are placed on the four white squares on the side of the board next to the player who is playing them; the fox is placed by *its* player on any white square of his choice. The moves are the same as in draughts i.e. diagonally, the geese being allowed to move forward only while the fox can move both back and forth. There is no 'jumping' over pieces and no taking. The geese are entitled to the first move, after which the moves are taken alternately. As long as the geese keep as far as possible in a straight line, making their forward movements at points furthest from the fox, the latter will not be able to break through, but much practice on the part of the geese is required before the secret of winning is mastered.

Go Bang: This game was the Victorian adaptation of the Japanese game of Go and was, in fact, played with identical equipment. For those who cannot quite grasp the immensities involved in the seeming simplicity of the Oriental game, Go Bang offers an interesting use for the Japanese boards and pieces that lie idle in so many cupboards. The game is simplicity itself.

It is played by two or four persons on a flat board divided into four hundred squares, twenty by twenty. To each of two players are allocated two hundred pieces of distinctive colour, or one hundred each to four players. The players set down a piece in any one of the unoccupied squares on any part of the board and the game is won by the first player to get five of his men together in a straight or diagonal line. A patented version of this game using a holed board and pegs for pieces was once available under the name of Peggity.

Draughts Go Bang: This version of Go Bang is played by two people on a draughts board with an ordinary set of draughts. Each player alternately places one of his pieces on *any* vacant square on the board until all the pieces are in place. If during this operation either player succeeds in getting five of his men in a line, vertically, horizontally or diagonally, he wins the game. This, however, rarely happens. Once all the pieces are on the board, each player alternately moves one of his pieces to any adjoining square with the object of forming a line of five of his men. Whichever player first succeeds in doing this says 'Go Bang' and is the winner.

Losing Draughts: This is not a difficult game and although it cannot be said to be quite so interesting as the regular game it is full of variety and makes a change from the original. The point of the game is for the player to bring up his men in a manner not only to force his opponent to take as many pieces as possible in one move, but also to arrange his own men to keep up a succession of losing hazards. It is, of course possible for a player with half-a-dozen men left on the board to compel his opponent to take them all with a single king; or, easier still, for a single king to move in such a way as to compel his adversary to give up his men one by one until he, the king, finds a way of committing suicide. Otherwise the rules of the game are exactly the same as those for regular draughts.

Nine Men's Morris: (2 players) This very ancient game was at one time played with stones as 'men' on a diagram marked out on the ground, usually outside the village inn or on the green. The game, once known as 'Fippeny Morrell', was neatly described in 1626 as, 'Thrice three stones, set in a crossed square, where he wins the game that can set his three in a row, and that is fippeny morrell I trow'.

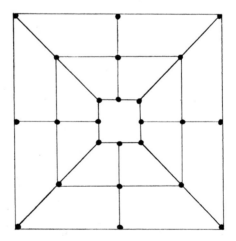

Nine Men's Morris boards can still be bought but can be just as easily drawn on paper. Two persons play, each having nine men or counters. Each player lays down a man alternately, one by one, upon the spots at the points of intersection of the lines, the object being to prevent the opponent from placing three of his pieces as to form a row. If a row is formed, the player who made it takes off one of his competitor's pieces from whatever part of the board he chooses but *not* from any row of three *unless* there is no other piece to remove.

When all nine men of both sides have been played the players move those that are left, backwards and forwards in any direction in which the lines run but only to an adjoining spot. In this way they continue to try to form 'threes' and still remove an opposing piece when they succeed in doing so. The player who takes off all his opponent's pieces wins the game.

French and English: A piece of paper about eighteen inches by twelve is marked out as the battlefield.

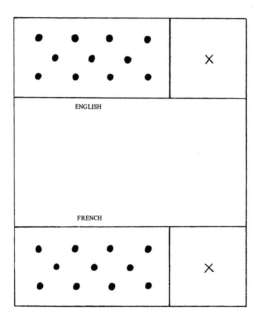

The players decide the order of play and the first (let us say he is English) puts the point of a pencil on the 'cannon' (marked with a cross) on the English side. He then closes his eyes, turns away his head and 'fires' at the enemy by drawing the pencil rapidly towards the other side. The pencil will leave a line and all men on the other side through which this line passes count as slain.

The track of the pencil may be straight or curved but any track containing an angle does not count. The players play alternately and the winner is he who first kills all the men on the other side.

Tit-Tat-Toe: Several people can play this old table game which in Georgian and Victorian times used to be played on a slate. It can now be just as well played with pencil and paper. A circle is drawn and divided into as many divisions as is thought necessary, sixteen generally being the least (*see* illustration below). The divisions are numbered, the centre containing a higher number than any in the divisions, usually 25 or 50. Each player has a square on which to record the numbers he obtains. A space on the board is allotted to 'Old Nick'. The players alternately take a pencil in their hand, holding it point down on division 1. They then shut their eyes and tap the pencil around the ring, making one tap for each word of the following rhyme which they recite aloud.

> Tit, tat, toe, my first go,
> Three jolly butcher boys all in a row.
> Stick one up, stick one down,
> Stick one in the old man's ground.

On the last word they keep the pencil where it has fallen, open their eyes and record, each in his own square, the number at which the pencil stopped. This number is now crossed out on the diagram to signify that it is taken and the other players proceed in

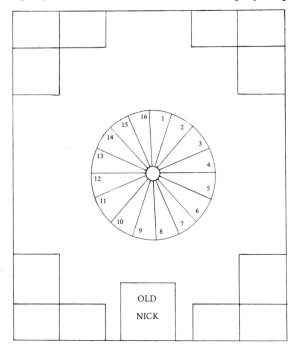

the same manner. The process is repeated until all the numbers have been taken, or until one puts his pencil in the centre ring. The scores are then added up, the highest being the winner. If all the figures are taken before the centre is touched, the game goes to 'Old Nick'. If one player puts his pencil in a division already taken, he records nothing and loses that turn; this is also the case if, on the last word of the verse, the pencil is found to be on a line or outside the circle.

Coronet: This game is played on a board which is simple to draw (*see* below). It should be made large enough for each of the six compartments to contain eight counters which may bear a real or nominal value. The game can, of course, be played with coins.

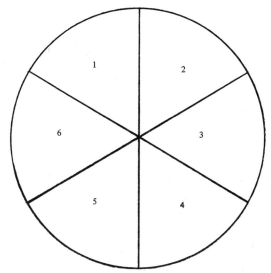

Each player chooses a compartment of the circle and deposits eight counters therein. The player who has the 'Six' compartment throws a die, the others throw in rotation and whatever number is thrown, the owner of that compartment receives four counters (or coins) – two from the compartment on his left, and two from that on his right.

Should one of the players lose all the eight counters staked before the end of the game he may, if he wishes, stake eight fresh counters and the game proceeds as before. If, on the other hand, he decides not to stake further counters, then any other player may claim that compartment by staking eight counters upon it. Should no one occupy a compartment it is considered non-existent and if its number should come up the die is cast again.

In the event of a blank compartment, the players receive winnings from the nearest right- or left-hand compartment.

The game is won by the player who first increases his eight counters to eighteen or more and, as the winner, he receives one counter from each player.

C. DOMINO GAMES

Dominoes are little flat pieces of wood, bone, ivory or (in today's form) plastic. The face of each 'card' forms a double square, and each square, except those which are left blank, bears a number of dots, known as 'pips' ranging from one to six. The full set consists of twenty-eight cards, ranging from double-six to double-blank:

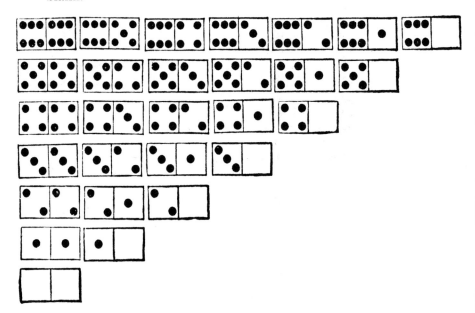

It will be seen that the set consists, in various combinations, of eight blanks, eight ones (or aces), eight twos (or deuces), eight threes (or trays), eight fours, fives and sixes – every number, therefore, being equally represented. In naming a given domino, the higher number is always mentioned first, as six-five, tray-deuce, deuce-ace etc. The principle of most domino games is the placing or 'posing' of cards by each player alternately, so as to 'follow suit', i.e. in such manner that one end of the card last placed must correspond in number with the *outer* end of one of those already on the table, the corresponding numbers being placed in juxtaposition.

The shuffling of the cards is common to all domino games. This is done by turning them face-downwards on the table and mixing them up with the fingers. Each player has the right to join in this operation. The right to first *pose* (i.e. to lay down the first card) is then decided by each player turning up one domino, the drawer of the lowest number of pips winning preference. The dominoes thus used are returned to the pack which is then re-shuffled. Each player then draws at random from the pack until he has in hand the number appropriate to the game to be played.

The Block Game: This is the parent of all domino games, for two players. Each player draws seven cards. The leader (A) poses face upwards any card he pleases – for example, the six-five. His opponent (B) must play to this a second card, also having at one of its ends either a six or a five – the six or five end must be placed touching the corresponding end of the card already played. Say he plays a six-three – the two cards will then be:

A. 1.   **B. 1.**

A must now play either a five or a three. We will suppose that he plays double-five. (It is usual to place a double crosswise to the line.) This does not alter the position and B in turn can only play a card which has a five or a three. He plays, say, five-four, which he places against A's double. A continues with, say, four-ace, and B (at the opposite end) with three-four. The game will then stand as below:

A. 2.

A. 3.   **B. 2.**   **A. 1.**   **B. 1.**   **B. 3.**

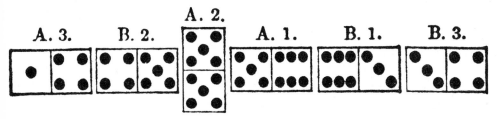

It is now A's turn and we will suppose that he has neither a four nor an ace. He is consequently 'blocked' and B plays again. If he can maintain the block he will, of course, do so and we will suppose that he does so by playing double-four leaving A still unable to play. B continues with three-ace. A responds with three-five and B with five-ace.

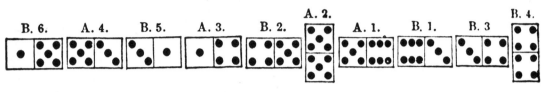

Now we will suppose that neither player has a four or an ace left. Both are therefore 'blocked' and the hand is at an end. The players add together the total pips they still hold unplayed and he with the lowest number wins. This is the simplest way of scoring and when it is used a rubber of three games is usually played. Sometimes the game is played for a given number, say 50, 60 or 100, 'up'. In this case the holder of the smaller number scores the *difference* of points between himself and his adversary, i.e. if A has twelve pips left in his hand and B seven, the latter scores five towards game. When one player scores 'domino', i.e. he gets rid of all his cards, he scores the whole number of points left in the hand of his adversary.

Sebastopol or *The Fortress:* This is a four-handed version of the Block Game, each combatant playing independently. All the dominoes are divided and the holder of the double-six leads, playing that card. Each player in rotation must play a six or pass. The first and second six played are placed above and below the double, the other two at right angles to it, forming a cross:

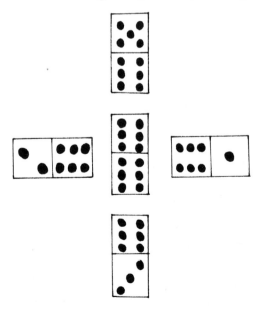

After the first round, a player may play to any number that is open and the game proceeds as in the Block Game.

Matadors: The two players each draw seven cards, and the one who has the highest double begins. The object in this case is not to *match* the end number, but to play to it such a number as, added to it, will make seven. Thus to a five a two must be played, to a four a three, to six an ace, and so on. If the player whose turn it is cannot make seven, he is blocked, and must draw from the reserve until he gets a card that will allow him to play. As six is the highest point, a blank would create an absolute block. To prevent such a block, four dominoes, the six-ace, the five-two, the four-three (i.e. all those which in themselves make seven) and the double blank are known as matadors, and may not only be played to a blank but, by special licence, to any number whatsoever. If a player is blocked, he must continue to draw until he can play, subject to the rule that at least two dominoes must be left undrawn.

Although a matador may be played to any number, the converse does not hold. The opposing player can follow only with a card making seven with one of the ends of the matador. Thus to a six-ace a player must play either a one or a six, to a five-deuce, either a two or a five, and so on. Sometimes matadors are placed crosswise at the end of the line, and it is left open to the adversary to play to either end of it, as he pleases; the more usual practice is to allow the player of a matador to place it as he thinks best, in which case his opponent can only play to the exposed end. Let us suppose that A (the leader) plays a double-six, and B replies with ace-blank. A, if he plays to the blank, must do so with a matador. He plays, say, five-two. He may place it either as shown in Fig. A or in Fig. B. B, in the first case must now play either an ace or a five; in the second case, an ace or a two.
It is customary, although not compulsory, to place a matador at

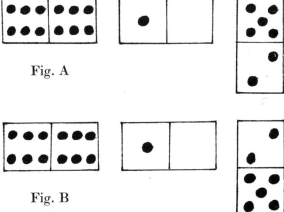

Fig. A

Fig. B

right angles to the rest of the line, as shown in the figures.

In play a double counts only as a single piece. Thus double-six is merely regarded as six, and an ace must be played to it. But in reckoning up the score, which is done on the same principle as in the Block Game, the full number of pips is counted. Should the game become blocked while one of the players still holds a matador, he can, of course, open it, but he is not bound to do so if he considers that it is in his interest for the game to end at that point.

Blanks are very useful in this game, as only matadors can be played to them. The play of a blank, therefore, will either leave the adversary blocked, or compel him to part with a matador. It is, on the other hand, unsafe to play a blank unless the player himself has one or more matadors in his hand for otherwise the blank may operate to his disadvantage.

Domino Loo: (3 or 4 players) This is a version of the card game of the same name but played with dominoes. We suggest that those who are unfamiliar with the card game should look at the account given on page 109 before attempting to play Domino Loo.

The game is best played by three or four players, each playing five dominoes and each putting up a stake, the amount of which is divisible by five. The dealer puts up a double stake. The cards are regarded as of six different suits – the six suit, the five suit, and so on down to the ace suit. The player of any given card has the right to decide to which of the two suits it shall be considered to belong.

The cards are shuffled and the dealer gives five to each player. As in the card game, he also deals an extra hand known as 'miss'. He then turns up one card from the stock to decide trumps. This is governed by the *heavier* end of the turn-up card. Thus, if six-three is turned up, 'sixes' will be the trump suit. If a double is turned up, then that number will be trumps.

Any player dissatisfied with his hand (beginning with the elder hand i.e. the one on the left of the dealer) has, in turn, the option of taking 'miss' – that is, he takes up the extra hand in place of his own which he discards. The dealer has the right to take the turned-up (trump) card into his hand, discarding (without showing) any card from his hand.

The elder hand now leads, placing the card face upwards on the table, and at the same time naming it, the order in which he names the point determining the suit to which he wishes it to belong. Thus, if he plays five-four, and so announces it, the card belongs to the five suit, but if he calls it four-five it belongs to the four suit. The other players must follow suit, if able, and the highest wins the trick. If a player cannot follow suit, he may trump i.e. play a card of the trump suit or he may discard a card of any other suit. A player is not bound to head the trick (that is, win it if he can), or to trump it, but if he holds two trumps, he is bound to play one of them; and, after winning a trick, he is bound to lead a trump if able to do so.

At the end of the game, each trick won entitles the player to a fifth of the amount in the pool. A player winning no trick is looed, and has to contribute to the pool, as may be agreed, either the original stake or the amount already in the pool (subject to a limit agreed on beforehand). If each player takes a trick, so that no one is looed, each contributes the same stake as at first to form a new pool.

Each player has the option of 'passing' i.e. throwing in his hand altogether, in which case he cannot be looed. Any one taking 'miss' is bound to play. If all pass except the dealer, he is entitled to the pool. If all save one have passed, the dealer *must* play, with the option of taking 'miss' if it is still available, but he may do so either on his own account or 'for the pool'. In the latter case he cannot be looed, but the value of any tricks he may make remain in the pool to await the result of the next round. He may look at his hand before declaring what he proposes to do, but if he takes and looks at 'miss' without previously announcing his decision, he is bound to play on his own account.

The Bergen Game: (2 players) Each player draws six cards. The player holding the lowest double (in this game known as a 'double-header') leads, and scores two. If neither player holds a double they each alternately draw another card until a double-header appears. This is then played and scores two. The second player must follow suit or, if he cannot, must draw another card. If this does not enable him to follow suit he says 'Go' and the leader in turn plays or draws from the pool. Whenever a player succeeds in making both ends of the line alike, say, two fives, or two sixes, this is also counted as a double-header and the player scores two. Doubles (except the first one played) have no scoring value in themselves, but if one of the ends of the line be a double, and the next player's card makes the other end of the same value, or if a double is played at either end of an existing double-header, it is known as a triple-header, and counts three points.

Fifteen points constitutes game, the player making domino (i.e. the first to exhaust his hand) scores one. If the game ends through both players being blocked, the player holding the smallest number of pips, and no double, is the winner of that hand and scores one. If, however, the holder of the smallest hand holds a double and his opponent does not, the latter is the winner. If both hold doubles, the player with the smallest number of doubles, irrespective of denomination, wins. If each has a double, the holder of the smaller one wins. When a player is within two points of game, a double-header will not give him game but will only count as one. Similarly, when a player is within three of winning, a triple-header counts only as two.

d. SOLITAIRE

This ancient game, once a feature in every parlour, is now enjoying a come-back. Sets of solitaire, consisting of a board and thirty-three marbles, can be bought at any good toy-shop. The board is marked with 33 holes arranged as follows:

		1	2	3		
		4	5	6		
7	8	9	10	11	12	13
14	15	16	17	18	19	20
21	22	23	24	25	26	27
		28	29	30		
		31	32	33		

With all the marbles except one placed on the board the object of the game is to clear the board of every marble but one, leaving this last in the space first made vacant. The marbles are removed by being passed over by an adjacent marble rather as in draughts except that the marbles move vertically or horizontally in either direction. They cannot move diagonally. Thus if spaces numbers 3 and 9 are vacant, the marble at number 1 may remove marble 2 by jumping over it to space 3 or, alternatively, it may remove marble 4 by jumping to space 9. The player should pose his own problems and then try to solve them, but the keys to three problems are given here to demonstrate the general principles and systems of play that can be applied to the game. For the sake of brevity, the moves only are given, it being always remembered that a marble passed over by another is removed from the board and that no piece can move unless it *does* so take another piece.

Problem No. 1 (This is the most usually played game and is known as the Centre Hole game.)

Remove the centre marble, No. 17

1:	5	to	17
2:	12	to	10
3:	3	to	11
4:	18	to	6
5:	1	to	3, and again, on to 11
6:	30	to	18
7:	27	to	25
8:	24	to	26
9:	13	to	27, and again, on to 25
10:	22	to	24
11:	31	to	23
12:	16	to	28
13:	33	to	31, and again, to 23
14:	4	to	16
15:	7	to	9
16:	10	to	8
17:	21	to	7, and again, to 9
18:	24	to	10, and again, to 8, 22, 24 and 26
19:	19	to	17
20:	16	to	18
21:	11	to	25
22:	26	to	24
23:	29	to	17, which was the starting point.

Problem No. 2

Remove the ball at 14

1:	16	to	14
2:	4	to	16
3:	17	to	15
4:	6	to	4
5:	29	to	17, and again, on to 5
6:	2	to	10
7:	18	to	6
8:	3	to	11
9:	20	to	18, and again, on to 6
10:	13	to	11
11:	6	to	18
12:	26	to	24
13:	33	to	25
14:	24	to	26
15:	27	to	25
16:	31	to	33
17:	18	to	30
18:	33	to	25
19:	22	to	24
20:	25	to	23
21:	7	to	9
22:	10	to	8
23:	1	to	9
24:	28	to	16, and again, on to 4
25:	21	to	7, and again, on to 9
26:	4	to	16, and again, on to 14, the starting point.

The above problem may be adapted to clear the board starting with ball 2, ball 20 or ball 32.

Problem No. 3

Remove the ball at 1

1:	9	to	1
2:	7	to	9
3:	10	to	8
4:	21	to	7
5:	7	to	9
6:	22	to	8
7:	8	to	10
8:	6	to	4
9:	1	to	9

10:	18	to	6
11:	3	to	11
12:	20	to	18
13:	18	to	6
14:	30	to	18
15:	27	to	25
16:	24	to	26
17:	28	to	30
18:	33	to	25
19:	18	to	30
20:	31	to	33
21:	33	to	25
22:	26	to	24
23:	16	to	18
24:	23	to	25
25:	25	to	11
26:	6	to	18
27:	13	to	11
28:	18	to	6
29:	9	to	11
30:	11	to	3
31:	3	to	1, the starting point.

This problem can be adapted when using any of the corner balls as starters.

If the above problems are studied it will be seen that it is possible to start and end a game on any point of the board selected. When this skill is obtained the player will be able to set himself (and solve) problems that involve leaving a given number of balls in specified positions. When the game is thoroughly mastered any desired combination can be played for.

4 Card Games

THE HISTORY of playing cards has long been of interest to scholars and yet it is still not known where and when they originated. We do know, however, that for nearly six hundred years, good round card games have provided excellent family entertainment in Europe and that it will take something far more powerful than radio and television to make card-playing a thing of the past.

As a social pastime, card-playing (along with other indoor recreations in general) reached its peak in the nineteenth century. Faced with the isolation of living in crowded towns, with every evening free and with the newly invented gaslight discouraging early retirement, people found card-playing an absorbing pastime for the evenings – especially in the winter months. Indeed, many card games were invented in the 1860s.

The close connexion between the introduction of gaslighting and the increase in popularity of card-playing is interesting. In 1813, the foundation was laid for the London and Westminster Gas Company, soon to become the famous Gas, Light and Coke Company. It built three manufacturing stations in London and laid 15 miles of mains. By 1861, so many gas companies had sprung up in the metropolis and other large towns in Great Britain that they were officially recorded as being 'innumerable'. During that same period, 'innumerable' card games had been invented or devised, some being completely original, others based on older games. They include Écarté, Newmarket, Euchre, Poker, Bézique, Bridge and all the derivations and varieties of the latter game. In addition, many of the older games, such as Matrimony, Brag, Cassino, Faro, Speculation and Pope Joan were revived.

In his *magnum opus* of Victorian parlour pastimes *Card and Table Games*, 'Professor' Louis Hoffman devotes no less than 327 pages of close type to describing some of the card games popular in the latter part of the nineteenth century, and this he does without deigning to give an inch of space to such games as Old Maid, Donkey or any other children's favourites. Compiling this section has therefore been a matter of careful selection to include those games which will still have appeal. This selection ranges from the simplest children's games to some in which pennies may inflate to pounds with extraordinary and alarming rapidity.

The game of Whist, together with all its variations and relations has not been included, for it is a subject that requires a book to itself. Also excluded are the other 'serious' games such as Poker and Cribbage and 'professional' gambling games like Baccarat, although all these were in vogue during our period. However, some of the games described are based on Whist and, for those who have no knowledge of this game, the basic principles are explained under German Whist (p. 104).

a. CARD GAMES FOR FUN

Snap: (2–6 players) This ever-popular card game is ideal for a mixture of ages, although often a cause of bitterness for the older players who tend to lose repeatedly. From two to six players may take part, two packs of cards being used if the number of players is four or more.

All the cards are shuffled and dealt face down to each player. The hands are taken up but are kept face down and the players must not look at them. Starting from the dealer's left, each player in turn takes the top card from his hand and lays it face up in front of him. This play continues until two of the exposed cards coincide – i.e, two Kings, two tens, two twos etc. When this happens, the owners of the two cards have the opportunity (presuming, that is, that they have noticed the phenomenon) of calling 'SNAP!' and the first of the two to do so takes up all the cards played by both. It should be noted that the other players do not have the right of calling but must wait until one of their cards coincides with another. The game continues until eventually one player holds all the cards. If a player is left with only one card, this remains on the table until it coincides with another when its holder must call 'snap' first or lose his card and drop out of the game altogether.

Animal Grab: (3–6 players) This is another form of Snap. Each player is given the distinctive cry of some animal – dog, cat, sheep, cow etc. – and the game is then played in the usual way, except that when two players turn up similar cards, instead of crying 'snap', they give the cry belonging to the *other* person. The tendency is for the players to give their own sound, or to search their memories for the noise belonging to the other person. The one who gives the right cry first wins the cards.

Grimace Snap: (3–6 players) In this game the rules of ordinary Snap are followed except that when two similar cards come up the players do not cry 'snap' but each endeavours to make the other laugh – to which end they may do anything but speak or touch each other. The first one to laugh loses his cards. The effect of this game is ludicrous.

Grab Cork or *Silent Snap:* (3–6 players) This is played like ordinary Snap except that when two cards are alike, instead of shouting 'snap', the players must try to secure a cork that is in the middle of the table. This is a most suitable game for the younger members of the family on Sunday afternoons, after lunch.

Old Maid: This simple card game is suitable for two or more players. A full pack of cards is used minus one of the Queens – any one may be removed. The cards are then shuffled and dealt to all the players until the pack is exhausted. Each player then looks at his hand and discards any pairs that it may contain. When all the pairs have been thrown out, the player on the left of the dealer offers his hand, face down, to the player on his left-hand side who draws any one card of his choice. If this card should pair with one already in his hand he discards that pair;

if not it remains in his hand with the rest of his cards. Either way, he then offers his hand to the player on his left.

In the course of the game all the cards will be paired and thrown out. It is the object of the game to try to pass the odd Queen to the next player for the holder of it at the end of the game is the Old Maid. With the variation of discarding not necessarily a Queen but any *unknown* card, the game gains an extra interest for no one has any idea of which card in the pack will make him or her the Old Maid.

Beggar-my-Neighbour or *Strip Jack Naked:* This game is suitable for two or more players. The pack is shuffled and one player deals out the entire pack equally. The player on the left of the dealer leads and the players each turn up a card in turn. When certain cards are turned up by a player, his neighbour must pay him a certain number of cards as forfeit: 1 card is paid for a Knave, 2 for a Queen, 3 for a King and 4 for an Ace. When payment is made, the player being paid picks up all the cards that have been laid down and puts them underneath those in his hand. If, however, while paying a forfeit, a player himself turns up an Ace, King, Queen or Knave he stops paying and is paid in turn by *his* neighbour. The game continues until all the cards are in the hand of one player – he is the winner. Any player who loses all his cards is out of the game.

Donkey: (6–13 players) This game is particularly suitable for children's parties when a little light relief is required. Ideally it is played by thirteen players, allowing the full pack to be distributed four to a player. If there are only twelve players, then all the twos are removed from the pack; for eleven players, twos and threes are removed, etc. The cards are then dealt, four to each player, and are held in the hand ready for play. On the word 'go' from the dealer all the players *simultaneously* take a card from their hands and pass it face down to the player on their left. This continues at speed, each player retaining the cards he requires to make up four of a kind and passing on those cards which he does not want. The moment one of the players obtains his four of a kind he lays them face up on the table, sits back and folds his arms. As soon as another player notices this he does the same. The last player to sit back is the loser of that round and he is given the letter 'D', the first letter of Donkey. If he should lose a second time he becomes DO, and the game continues until one player has lost six times, which, of course, makes him the DONKEY.

99

Fish or *Pelmanism:* This is a memory game, suitable for any number of players. With large numbers, two packs of cards may be used. The cards are shuffled and then laid out in rows face down on the table. The first player then turns up any two cards. If they make a pair he takes them up and puts them face down in front of him. This entitles him to a further turn and he turns up two more cards. If they are not a pair he turns them face down again and the turn passes to the player on his left. After the first few rounds, the positions of certain cards will become known to the players and those that remember them will collect the most pairs. When all the cards have been paired the player with the most is the winner.

The Seven Blows of Circumstance: (4 or more players) This is an exciting game and very suitable for parties as it will be enjoyed by all from the age of seven upwards. The Ace, two, three, four, five, six and seven of Hearts are taken from the pack and put on the table face up and in numerical order to form a circle. These are the Seven Blows of Circumstance and the centre of the ring is the pool. One card is then dealt to each player from the remainder of the pack and with it a small piece of paper bearing the player's name. The object of the game is to get possession of as low a card as possible (Ace counting low) for the player with the highest card has to put on a 'Blow' – that is, he must put his name-paper on the Ace of Hearts and, as the game proceeds, every time his card is the highest he must move his name one up, until, after the seven of Hearts is reached, he is 'submerged' in the pool. There he stays until the end of the game or until some other player speaks to him. A player in the pool may use any reasonable device to get another player to make the mistake of speaking to him and if he is successful he is taken out of the pool and can begin his 'life' afresh. The player that spoke to him is automatically raised to the seventh Blow of Circumstance.

After the cards have been dealt one to each player, the game proceeds as follows. The first player to have been dealt a card has the option of passing it (should he consider it to be too high) to his left-hand neighbour and receiving his in exchange. The first player must not look at this card (under penalty of adding a blow to his account) until all the other players have changed (or refused to change) their cards. The second player looks at the card dealt to him, or to the one received in exchange for it, and if he thinks it too high, he can pass it on in turn to Number 3. This goes on until all but the dealer have passed or exchanged. The dealer may exchange his card for a random one in the pack if he wishes. Then all the cards are turned up (all the players who have exchanged seeing their cards for the first time) and the player with the highest card has to take unto himself a Blow of Circumstance. Each player takes his turn as dealer and the game goes on until all the players but one are drowned in the pool, the survivor being the winner.

Ranter-Go-Round: (4 or more players) This is a more serious version of the previous game. Any number of players can join in but each must be supplied with three counters, or lives, the object of the game being to see which player will succeed in keeping at least one of his lives – high cards being desirable.

A full pack of cards is shuffled and one card is dealt face down to each player. The players look at their cards, and the one on the left of the dealer, if he thinks his card is too low, has the option of exchanging it with his left-hand neighbour. The neighbour must make the exchange if asked. He can then change cards with *his* left-hand neighbour, and so on round the table until the dealer is reached and, as he has no one with whom to exchange, he is allowed to take the top card from the remainder of the pack. The players one by one turn up their cards, starting with the player on the dealer's left and the possesser of the lowest card (Aces counting low) loses a life. If two players have cards of the same value and these cards are the lowest, the player who last turned up his card loses a life. The deal moves on to the next player.

If a player has given to his right-hand neighbour a card that is lower than the one received in the exchange, he will of course *stand* on that card, that is, he will not offer it in exchange to the player on *his* left for he will be well aware that at least *one* card lower than his is out. No player may exchange more than once. The vicissitudes of fortune in Ranter-Go-Round are remarkable. For instance a player may keep all his three lives until only he and one other are left in the game, and then he may lose them all in three successive rounds. On the other hand, a player may lose two lives very early on in the game and yet carry on with the remaining one to win.

Thank You: This is a game for four players and requires a good memory. The whole pack is dealt and the object is for each player to get as many sets of four as possible. The player to the left of the dealer asks any person he chooses for a certain card. He must not, however, ask for a card unless he holds at least one of the same value in his own hand.

For example, A, with a five of Clubs in his hand may ask C for the five of Hearts. If C has that card he must give it up to A and A may then proceed to ask him or any other player for another card and so on. If, however, a player is asked for a card he does not possess, the right of asking passes to him. In addition, if a player takes a card from another player he must say 'Thank you' *before* he touches it otherwise he loses to the other player both the card and the right of asking for another. In the case of A asking C for the five of Hearts and not saying 'Thank you', C will know that A possesses at least one five and has, therefore, a good chance of obtaining it.

At first it is entirely a matter of chance whether the right person is asked, but as the game progresses both memory and deduction play their parts. For instance, A has the 7 of Hearts and the 7 of Diamonds and B asks C for the 7 of Spades and is refused it. A then knows and must remember that B must have the 7 of Clubs and that D must have the 7 of Spades.

As soon as a player completes a set of four he lays it face down on the table in front of him. When all the cards are thus laid down the players aim at getting possession of the complete pack by asking each other for sets. This part of the game is played in the same way as the first part, the player who completed the last set being the first to ask. The same rule of saying 'Thank you' applies. The omission of these words may cost a player the game, for the player who passed the last set, if not thanked for it, may retaliate by demanding all the sets his opponent has collected.

The Book of Fate: (4–8 players) This is a unique card game for it involves not only forfeits but the possible exchange of numerous kisses. The president of the game takes a pack of cards and deals three to each player. He keeps the remainder himself; these he may consult when necessary although he has nothing to do with the game beyond superintending it. Each player conceals his cards from his neighbours. After dealing the president asks the player on his left: 'Have you read the Book of Fate?' The player replies, 'Yes, I have read the Book of Fate.' The president then asks, 'What did you read in the Book of Fate?' and the player replies, 'I read *so and so* (naming any card provided it is not in his own hand).' The president then consults the reserve pack and if the named card is found there the player naming it pays a forfeit. If not, the others examine their hands, and the one in whose hand it is found gives it up to the president. At this point the person naming the card and the one in whose hand it is found must, if they are of different sexes, exchange a kiss; otherwise both pay forfeits.

The game now proceeds thus. The person previously questioned now becomes the questioner and asks the player on his left 'Have you read the Book of Fate?' – and so on until all the cards have returned to the hands of the president.

Should anyone in the course of the game ask for a card that has already been dealt with, he must pay a forfeit. Consequently, to avoid disputes, the president should take care to keep apart from the rest of the pack the cards already asked for and to conceal them from the players so as to give no hint of what has gone before. It must be thoroughly understood that any card found in the hand of the player who asks for it is evidence of immense stupidity and a severe forfeit should be imposed. In the case of a gentleman, I'm In a Well (page 136) would be appropriate; in that of a lady, she should be compelled either to Run the Gauntlet (page 135) or Perform the Parrot (page 129).

Cheat: (3 or more players) A full pack of 52 cards is dealt equally to the players. Any cards remaining are placed face down in the centre of the table. When all the players have examined their cards, the player on the dealer's left leads any card face down on the table, naming its denomination. Thus, if his card is a 5, he must say 'five'. The next player must now play a 6 on top of the 5, again face down, and call 'six'. It is not necessary, however, for the card laid down to be the same as the number called. The play goes on, 7 follows 6, 8 follows 7 and so on. After a King, the next card declared is 'Ace'. Any one of the company is at liberty to challenge a player to show the last card played by calling out 'Cheat'. In this case, the player must show his card and if it is not what he claimed it to be he must pick up all the cards previously laid down on the table. If he proves himself honest, then his detractor must pick up the cards. After a challenge, the player to the left of the one challenged plays any card he likes to the table. It is legitimate to cheat also by playing two cards at once. The player who first gets rid of all his cards is the winner.

Truth: (4–8 players) Two packs of cards are required for this game, one of which is placed face down in front of the dealer, and the other dealt to the company including the dealer, card by card, until it is exhausted. The dealer then asks a question concerning the company, at the same time turning up a card from the undealt pack. Whatever card this is, the dealer calls for its counterpart from the players and the holder of it must reply to the question. Ridiculous personal questions create the most fun. Turning up the Queen of Hearts, for instance, the dealer may ask, 'Who is it that thinks they are the most good-looking person here?' The holder of the corresponding card must then stand up and admit his vanity. As a compensation for this, however, he (or she) is entitled to put the next question. As the question and answer cards are produced they are laid aside and the game proceeds until both packs are finished.

b. CARD GAMES FOR MONEY

German Whist: (2 players) This is the simplest game of Whist and it incorporates all the basic principles of Whist proper. The game is for two players only. The cards rank as follows (Ace high): Ace, King, Queen, Knave, ten, nine, eight, seven, six, five, four, three, two. The four suits are equal in value but the suit that is 'turned up' as *trumps* has precedence over the other suits. When playing for tricks each player *must* (providing he is able) follow suit. If he cannot follow suit the player may, if the card led is not a trump, play a trump (in which case he wins the trick) or 'throw away', that is play a card that is not a trump and lose the trick irrespective of the value of the card he plays.

The players cut for deal, the highest card winning, and the dealer gives, one by one, thirteen cards to his opponent and himself. The remainder of the pack, known as the stock, is then laid face down on the table and the top card is turned up to determine the trump suit. This 'turn up' card is now played for as follows. The non-dealer selects any card from his hand and lays it face up on the table. The dealer now plays to that card according to the rules above, following suit if he can. Whoever plays the highest card takes the trick and the 'turn up' card. The trick he lays face down on the table beside him, the 'turn-up' card he adds to his hand. The loser of the trick takes the next card from the stock and adds it to *his* hand. The next card on the stock is turned up and played for in the same way, remembering that the first 'turn-up' determines trumps for the whole of the hand. The winner of a trick takes the lead for the next. When the twenty-six cards in the stock are exhausted, the play for tricks continues until no cards remain in the players' hands. The tricks are then counted and the player with the greater number scores the difference between his tricks and his opponent's (i.e. if a player makes 16 tricks and his opponent 10, he scores 6 points). A score limit, e.g. 50 points, should be set.

Bézique: This is a game for two players and, on its introduction to England in 1861, it enjoyed increasing popularity. The game is played with two Piquet packs (i.e. two packs from each of which the twos, threes, fours, fives and sixes have been removed). The two packs are shuffled together. (If four play, four packs must be used.)

After shuffling and cutting, the dealer gives eight cards (by three, two and three) to each player. The remainder of the pack – the talon – is left on the table and the top card is turned up to one side for trumps. If this turn-up card is a seven, the dealer scores 10.

The game now begins – the play of each hand being in two parts: first, each player plays a card from his hand, taking in exchange a card from the pack until this is exhausted; second, the eight cards which remain to each player are played out under different scoring conditions.

The preliminary play is as follows. The non-dealer leads to the first trick, to which the dealer will then play a card. The winner of the trick takes the top card from the talon (this is not the turn-up trump card), his opponent takes the next card. Play continues until this pile is exhausted. After the first turn-up card, the cards on the talon are left face down.

The value of the cards in making the tricks is as follows: Ace, ten, King, Queen, Knave, nine, eight, seven. In this preliminary part of the play there is no need to follow suit. The only objects of taking tricks at this stage of the game are (*a*) to cash in on Aces and tens – any Ace or ten included in a trick scores 10 for the winner of it; and (*b*) to make a Declaration. A Declaration can only be made by a player immediately after taking a trick. It consists in laying the appropriate cards face up on the table and mentioning the scoring combination claimed. A card that has been declared stays on the table until it is played. The exposed cards are led or played to a trick on the table in exactly the same way as cards in the hand. A Declaration is scored as it is claimed. They are as follows:

Common Marriage (King and Queen of any suit other than trumps) 20 points

Royal Marriage (King and Queen of the trump suit) 40 points

Bézique (Queen of Spades and Knave of Diamonds) 40 points

Four Knaves 40 points

Four Queens 60 points

Four Kings 80 points

Four Aces 100 points

Sequence (Ace, ten, King, Queen, Knave of the trump suit) 250 points

Double Bézique (both Queens of Spades and both Knaves of Diamonds) 500 points

As mentioned above, any Ace or ten included in tricks scores 10 points for the winner of the trick.

Finally, a player holding the seven of trumps in his hand may, immediately after taking a trick, exchange it for the turned-up trump card. Exchanging the seven ranks as a Declaration and another Declaration cannot be made at the same time.

Only one Declaration can be made at a time. Thus a player cannot put down a trump Sequence and score both for the Sequence and for a Royal Marriage.

The first stage of the game goes on until there are only two cards left which are not in the possession of the players i.e. the bottom card of the pack and the card turned up to indicate the trump suit (or the seven which has been exchanged for it). The winner of the last trick takes the bottom card and the loser takes the turn-up card.

The second part of the play is sometimes called the 'Play-Off'. Each player takes into his hand any exposed cards he has on the table and the eight tricks are played out. At this stage, a player must follow suit; if he cannot do this, he may trump or discard. No Declarations can be made but players continue to score 10 points for Aces or tens won in tricks. The scores are added up and game is usually taken to be 1,000 points.

Euchre: This game is still very popular in the United States and can be played by two, three or four players. It is played with a Piquet pack of 32 cards, i.e. with all cards below seven (Ace counting high) removed. The cards rank as in Whist, except that the Knave of trumps, known as the Right Bower, and the Knave of the suit of the same colour, the Left Bower, take temporary precedence over all other cards. Thus, when Hearts are trumps the cards rank as follows: Knave of Hearts, Knave of Diamonds, Ace, King, Queen, ten, nine, eight and seven of Hearts. The Left Bower is considered for the time being to belong to the trump suit, so that if this card is led, the trump suit is played to it. A still higher trump is sometimes, by agreement, introduced. This is the Joker, known in Euchre as Best Bower and it takes precedence even over the Right Bower. If the Joker chances to be the 'turn-up' card, the card next in order decides the trump suit.

TWO-HANDED EUCHRE

The players having cut for deal, five cards are dealt (by twos and then threes, or *vice versa*) to each player. The eleventh card is turned up by way of trump. If the non-dealer thinks his hand good enough, with the suit of the turn-up card as trumps, to make three tricks, he says, referring to that card, 'I order it up'. This fixes that suit as trumps. The dealer discards the worst card of his own hand, placing it face down under the pack, and the turn-up card is then considered to form part of his hand. He does not, however, actually take it into his hand until the first trick has been played. If the non-dealer does not consider his hand good for three tricks, or is of the opinion that he would be likely to gain by a change of the trump suit, he says, 'I pass', and the dealer examines his own cards from the same point of view. If he thinks his hand is good enough with the existing trump suit to make three tricks, he says, 'I take it up', and proceeds to place, as before, one card under the pack. If he does not think his hand safe for three, he says, 'I turn it down', and places the turn-up card below the rest of the pack. This annuls the trump suit, and the non-dealer now has the option of saying what suit shall be trumps. He considers what will best suit his hand, and says, 'Make it Hearts (or whichever suit is best)', accordingly. If he decides to 'make it' *of the same colour* as the previous turn-up card (e.g. Spades in place of Clubs, or Hearts in place of Diamonds), he is said to 'make it next'. If otherwise, to 'cross the suit'. If, even with the privilege of making the trump what he pleases, he doubts his ability to win three tricks, he again 'passes', and the dealer 'makes it' what best suits him. If he too has such a bad hand that he thinks it safer to 'pass' again, the cards are thrown up, and the deal passes.

The trump suit having been 'made' by the one or the other player, the non-dealer leads a card and the dealer plays to it. The second player must follow suit if he can, subject to the qualification that (as already stated) if the Left Bower be led, a trump must be played to it. The higher card wins and the winner of the trick leads to the next.

The player who has 'ordered up', 'taken up' (save in obedience to order), or 'made' the trump, has thereby tacitly undertaken to win at least three tricks. If he makes less than this number he is 'euchred', and his opponent scores two. If he makes three tricks he wins 'the point', and scores one. Four tricks are no better than three, but if he makes all five he wins a 'march', which scores two. The non-challenging player is not under any obligation to win, but scores if his adversary fails to do so. A score of five points constitutes 'Game'.

FOUR-HANDED EUCHRE

Where four players take part, two play in partnership against the other two, partners facing each other. Five cards are dealt to each, and the twenty-first is turned up by way of trump. The elder hand (to the left of the dealer) declares whether he will 'order up' the trump card or pass. If the latter, the option passes to the dealer's partner; but he expresses his position differently, as he is playing with a partner. If he thinks his hand good for two or more tricks he says, 'I assist'. This is considered a call to his partner (the dealer) to take up the trump, which he does accordingly, having no choice in the matter. If the second player passes, the option rests with the third player, who 'orders it up' or passes, as his hand may warrant. In the later case the dealer decides for himself whether to take it up or to turn it down. If the trump has either been ordered up or taken up voluntarily by the dealer, the play proceeds as in the two-handed game. If, on the other hand, the dealer 'turns it down', the players, beginning with the elder hand, are invited in succession to 'make it' what they please; the challenging party in either case being bound, in conjunction with his partner, to make three tricks, under penalty of being euchred.

A player with an unusually strong hand may elect to 'go alone'. In such a case, his partner turns his cards face down on the table, and leaves the 'lone hand', as he is termed, to play the game singly against the two opponents. If a player 'going alone' manages to win all five tricks, he scores *four* (instead of two for the 'march'); but if he makes three or four tricks only, he scores one for the point in the ordinary manner.

THREE-HANDED EUCHRE

In this form of the game each plays for his own hand. The value of the march and point are the same as in the two-handed game, but if the challenging player is euchred, each of his adversaries scores two points. If this should carry them both 'out', the elder hand is the winner. To avoid this, which is hardly a satisfactory termination for the younger hand, another method of scoring is sometimes adopted, the points for the euchre being *deducted* from the score of the euchred player, who is 'set back' accordingly. Should he have made no points towards game, he is considered to owe the points for the euchre; so that a player, standing at love when euchred, has seven points to make before he can win.

Marking the Score: Methods of scoring at Euchre are unusual. The score is usually kept by means of spare playing cards, a three and a four (of any suit) being used by each side. The 'three' face upwards, with the 'four' turned down upon it, indicates *one* (however many pips may chance to be exposed). The 'four' face upwards, with the 'three' turned down upon it, indicates *two*. The face of the 'three' being uppermost counts *three*; and the face of the 'four' being uppermost counts *four*.

Another method of keeping the score is by means of a cross chalked at the outset of the game on the table beside each player. 'One' is scored by rubbing out the centre of the cross, leaving the four arms still standing, and these in turn are rubbed out, one for each point which the player becomes entitled to score.

Loo: (4–8 players) In 1675, Wycherley wrote in *The Country Wife*:

> They may kiss the cards at Piquet, Hombre, Lu,
> And so he thought to kiss the Lady too.

So, clearly, Loo was already well established in the seventeenth century. During the nineteenth century it enjoyed greater popularity than perhaps any other round game although towards the end of the century it began to be superseded by Napoleon, Whist and Poker. There is no limit to the number of players, but six or seven make the better game. There are many versions of the game but only the two leading varieties, known as Three-Card and Five-Card Loo, are dealt with here.

THREE-CARD LOO

The full pack is used, the cards ranking as in Whist. The dealer places an agreed number of his counters (either three or some multiple of three) in the pool. Sometimes each player contributes an agreed amount to start the pool, but this is a matter of arrangement. Three cards are then dealt, one by one, to each player, with an extra hand, known as 'miss'. The card next following is then turned up and fixes the trump suit. The dealer then asks each player in succession, beginning with the elder hand, whether he will play or 'take miss'. If he holds a good hand, he will elect to play it, otherwise he has the option of either 'taking miss', i.e. taking the extra hand in place of his own, or of passing, i.e. throwing up his hand altogether for that round. If miss is declined, the same offer is made to the next player but as soon as miss is taken, the remaining players have only two alternatives; either to play the hand they hold, or to pass. A player who has taken miss is bound to play. The cards he has discarded together with those of any players who pass, are thrown face downwards in the middle of the table and no player may look at them.

Should one player take miss and all the rest throw in their cards, he is entitled to the pool. Should only one player declare to play, and he has not taken miss, the dealer may play either his own cards or take miss on his own account, but if he does not care to do either, he is bound to take miss and to play on behalf of the pool i.e. the proceeds of any tricks he may make must remain in the pool to await the result of the next round. In the event of all save the dealer passing the dealer is entitled to the pool.

The elder hand of those who have declared to play now leads a card, but he is subject to certain rules. If he has two trumps he must lead one of them. If he holds the Ace of trumps he is bound to lead it, or if an Ace be turned up, and he holds the King of the same suit, he is bound to lead the latter. If only two persons have declared to play, and the elder player holds two or more trumps, he must lead the *highest* unless his highest trumps are in sequence or of equal value (for instance, where a player holds the seven and nine of trumps, the eight having been turned up; the seven and nine are then of equal value) when he may lead either of them. With more than three declared players the last-mentioned rule does not apply.

The other players play in rotation to the card led, subject to these rules. Each player must follow suit if possible, and he must 'head the trick' i.e. he must play a higher card to it, if he is able to do so. If unable to follow suit, he is bound to trump, or if the trick be already trumped he must over-trump if he possibly can. The winner of each trick leads to the next. He is under the same obligations as the original leader, and is further bound to lead a trump, if he has one.

When the hand has been played out, the pool is divided, in the proportion of one third to each trick. Suppose, for instance, that five players have played; that one of them has taken two, and another one trick. The first takes two-thirds and the second one-third of the pool. The remaining three players are 'looed' i.e. they must each pay to the pool the same amount that was originally placed there. These 'loos', with a like contribution from the new dealer, form the pool for the next hand. It may happen that only three players declare to play, and that each of them takes one trick. In such a case, no one is looed, and the only fund to form the pool for the next round is the contribution of the dealer (plus the agreed contribution, if any, of the other players). The next hand in such a case is known as a single, and it is usual in such a case to make what is called a 'force' or a 'must', meaning that everyone, whatever his cards, is bound to play. This necessarily produces some loos and consequently a pool for the next hand. In the case of a 'must', there is no miss. In circles in which the gambling interest of Loo is the main one, the payment for a loo is sometimes made equal to the amount which may chance to be in the pool at that particular time. This form of Loo is known as Unlimited Loo for the amount of a loo tends consequently to increase, until the occurrence of a single (i.e. three players only declaring to play and each taking one trick) brings it back to its normal proportions. In Unlimited Loo pence grow to pounds with startling rapidity and the game should be avoided by prudent players unless a reasonable maximum is fixed, beyond which no advance is permitted.

FIVE-CARD LOO

In this game five cards are dealt to each player, the card next following being turned up for the trump suit. There are, therefore, five tricks to be played for and contributions to the pool are made divisible by five accordingly. In the five card version there is no 'miss' but each player, beginning with the elder hand, is entitled to discard as many cards as he pleases, the dealer replacing them with a like number from the stock. Each player has the option either to play or pass but once having drawn new cards he is bound to play.

In this version of the game the Knave of Clubs, known as 'Pam', is made into a sort of paramount trump and takes precedence even over the Ace of trumps. The rules as to leading, following suit and 'heading the trick' are the same as in the three-card game. If, however, the Ace of trumps be led, and the holder says, as he plays it, 'Pam, be civil', then the holder of Pam is bound to pass the trick and not play Pam unless he cannot follow suit.

Special value in this game is given to a flush i.e. five cards of the same suit, or four cards of the same suit and Pam. The holder of such a hand at once turns up his hand and 'looes the board', i.e. he wins every trick as of right, without playing his hand. No one, in this case, is allowed to throw in his hand, and all save the holder of the flush are looed. A flush of trumps has priority over one in a plain suit; in the case of two flushes in trumps, or two in plain suits, the better cards win. The holder of the losing flush, or of Pam, if in the hand of one of the losers, is exempt from payment. In all other respects the game is the same as Three-Card Loo.

Lansquenet: This is a game of considerable antiquity. It was popular in the Middle Ages with the German mercenaries known as *lansquenets*. It is essentially a gambling game of pure chance.

Any number of persons may play. A full pack of 52 cards is usually used, but sometimes two packs are used, shuffled together.

After the shuffle, the dealer lays two cards face up by his left hand – these are known as 'hand' cards. He then deals a card for himself and a fourth card, known as the *réjouissance* card, in the

111

centre of the table. It is on this last card that the rest of the players bet. If either the dealer's card or the *réjouissance* card is of the same denomination as either of the hand cards, it must be put with them and another card dealt in its place, because all bets must be made on single cards.

When all the players have placed their stakes on the *réjouissance* card, the dealer must cover them with equal stakes. He then turns up the next card of the pack. If this card matches the *réjouissance* card, the dealer takes all that is staked on it. If it matches his own card, he loses all the bets on the *réjouissance* card. If this card matches neither of these nor one of the hand cards, it is placed on the table and players may bet on it also. Another card is then dealt and the same procedure observed. As soon as the players' card is matched, the banker withdraws the pair but he may never withdraw his own. As has been said, all cards dealt that match the hand cards must be placed with them. The deal comes to an end when a card is turned up that matches the dealer's card. When this happens, the dealer pays all outstanding stakes and passes the deal to his left. If both the hand cards are paired before the dealer's own card is matched, the dealer may, if he chooses, have a second deal.

Napoleon: This is a game that can be played by any number of players from two to six – four to six being the ideal. It is played with a full pack of 52 cards which rank as in Whist. When the pack has been shuffled, the dealer (each player dealing in turn) deals out five cards to each player. The player on the left of the dealer now has the opportunity of 'calling', that is, of declaring how many tricks he thinks he can take with that hand. He may not call 'one', that is to say, that he will make one trick, but he may call 2, 3, 4, or Nap (5). In the event of this player deciding to pass, the player on his left has the option of the call and so on. When a call *is* made, the player on the left of the caller may, if he wishes, better that call, at which the first caller, or for that matter any of the other players, may better it further. The player who makes the highest call leads to the first trick. The first card he plays determines trumps.

The caller now plays against all the others while they try to prevent him from making the tricks he has declared to take. If the caller succeeds in his boast he receives an arranged sum from each of the other players. Should he fail, he pays each of them this sum. If the caller makes 'Nap' he receives double stakes from every one in the company.

In some circles there is a rule that when 'Nap' has been called the caller may draw a card from the top of the remains of the pack and either keep it or return it. If he keeps it he discards another card from his hand.

Misère is sometimes introduced in Napoleon, that is the caller undertakes to lose every trick. Misère is reckoned in value as three points although below three in precedence of call.

Speculation: This is a game for any number of players. The full pack is used and each player is supplied with an equal number of counters. A certain agreed number are contributed by each player to form the pool, the dealer paying double. The cards rank as at Whist (Ace high). The dealer gives three cards face down to each player and no player must look at his cards until later. Any player doing so is fined for each card looked at. These counters are put in the pool. The top card of the remainder is turned up for trumps. This extra card becomes the dealer's property, in consideration of his double payments to the pool.

The object of the game is to hold the best trump among the cards dealt. Should the turn-up card be an Ace, the pool, as of right, goes to the dealer. If, otherwise, it is a fairly high one, say a ten or a court card, it becomes an object of speculation and the dealer may sell it to the highest bidder. He inquires 'Who buys?' and names his price in counters. If a purchaser is found he pays the agreed price to the pool and places the card face up on top of his own hand.

The player on the left of the purchaser then turns up his top card and if this is not a trump, the next player turns up a card and so on, until a higher trump than the first should appear. When this happens, the new card, if not kept by its owner, is given to the highest bidder. If the card is not a trump, it may be beaten by the highest card that is turned up of the same suit or by another trump. This in turn becomes an object of speculation and the owner of the highest trump exposed is exempt from turning up any other card until he has been beaten.

At the close of every round the pool is won by the player who holds the highest card of the trump suit. If the Ace of trumps is turned up, the round is concluded at once and its owner is the winner.

This buying and selling business is often carried on to a considerable extent. Sometimes players will sell their whole hands to each other, or a single card blind on the chance of its proving a winner. Sometimes the game is played with an extra hand being dealt and placed in the middle of the table for pool. At the end of the round this hand is examined and if a better card is found in it than that belonging to the winner, the pool is left undisturbed and added to the next new pool. In some circles, anyone turning up a five or a Knave pays one or more counters to the pool.

Pope Joan: (3 or more players) This once very popular game is played with a pack of 52 cards, from which the eight of Diamonds (for a reason which will presently appear) has been removed, and with a special board, consisting of a circular tray around a central pillar, divided into eight compartments, as shown below, respectively marked POPE (the nine of diamonds), MATRIMONY, INTRIGUE, ACE, KING, QUEEN, KNAVE and GAME. Matrimony signifies the combination in the same hand of the King and Queen of the trump suit; Intrigue that of Knave and Queen. The board is not essential to the game for a similar lay-out can be drawn on paper.

Each player is provided with an equal number of counters (say three or four dozen) each bearing an agreed value. The first dealer then 'dresses' the board, that is he distributes between the eight divisions fifteen counters from his own store as follows: six to Pope, two to Matrimony, two to Intrigue, and one each to Ace, King, Queen, Knave and Game. All the cards are then dealt out one by one but with an extra hand being dealt to the centre of the table. All players must hold an equal number of cards, any remaining being added to the extra hand on the table. The last card dealt (and this will be to the extra hand) is turned up as trumps. Should the turn-up card be Pope (nine of Diamonds), or an Ace, King, Queen or Knave, the dealer is entitled to all the counters in the corresponding compartments.

The player on the dealer's left then leads any card he pleases, at the same time naming it. Let us suppose it to be the three of Diamonds. The player holding the four plays it to the three, the players holding the five, six and seven play them in like manner. In any other suit it would be possible to continue with the eight but, as we have seen, the eight has been removed thus making the seven what is called a 'stop' card. That is, the run on that particular lead cannot be continued and the player of the seven is entitled to lead again. But besides the permanent removal of the eight of Diamonds it will be remembered that a certain number of other (unknown) cards were dealt as an extra hand and, not being in play, create other 'stop' cards. Let us suppose that the extra hand consists of the two, five and nine of Spades, the six and ten of Hearts, the Knave of Diamonds, and the King of Clubs. These, not being in circulation, make stop cards of those immediately preceding them (i.e. the Ace, four and eight of Spades, the five and nine of Hearts, the ten of Diamonds and the Queen of Clubs.) As play proceeds other cards will also become stops because the cards next following them have already been played. Thus, in the case above, with the three of Diamonds being led, the two of Diamonds becomes a stop and its holder should note that fact for his future guidance. All Kings are necessarily stops as they are counted as the highest cards of their suits.

Whenever, in the course of play, the Ace, King, Queen or Knave of the trump suit appears, the holder is entitled to all the counters in the corresponding compartment. Should King and Queen, or Queen and Knave fall from the same hand, the holder is entitled to the proceeds of Matrimony or Intrigue, as the case may be. Anyone playing Pope takes all the counters in that division. Unless actually played, the above cards have no value, except that the player holding Pope (unplayed) is exempted from paying for any surplus cards as will be explained.

The game proceeds as described until one of the players has played all his cards. This gives him Game and all the counters in that compartment and entitles him to receive from each other player one counter for each card such player may still hold in his hand, except for the holder of Pope who is exempt. If Pope has been played no exemption exists.

115

The skill of the player will be shown in his ability to note, on one hand, which of the cards are stops, and on the other, what cards cannot be led to, and which, therefore, should be got rid of as soon as possible. At the outset, the only *known* cards which cannot be led to are the four Aces, Pope and the next card above the turn-up (the next lower being a stop). But the list of stops increases as the game goes on. If, for instance, the nine of Hearts is known to be a stop because the ten is in the surplus hand, it is clear that the Knave cannot be led to and must itself be led in order to get rid of it.

Sequences are valuable, inasmuch as they enable the player to get rid of two, three or more cards simultaneously. Nearly as useful are alternate sequences such as seven, nine, Knave – the lowest, of course, being led. Pope, as we have seen, can only be played when its holder has the lead and it is usually wise, therefore, to do so at the first opportunity.

The unclaimed counters in each compartment are left to accumulate. In the case of Matrimony and Intrigue, a whole evening may occasionally pass without the necessary combinations being played from the same hand and these compartments may become very rich. The same applies to Pope, or one or more of the Ace, King, Queen and Knave compartments. The best method of disposing of any such counters at the close of the game is to deal a final round face up (without the surplus hand), the holder of Pope, and of the Ace, King, Queen and Knave of the *Diamond* suit being entitled to the counters in the corresponding compartments. The holder of the Queen takes in addition half the amount in Matrimony and in Intrigue, the remaining halves going to the holders of the King and Knave respectively.

Newmarket: (3–7 players) This is a simpler version of Pope Joan and there is no need for the board or elaborate lay-out. Instead, four 'luxury' cards from a spare pack are laid in a square in the centre of the table: the Ace of Spades, King of Hearts, Queen of Clubs, and Knave of Diamonds. The game is then played with a full pack from which the eight of Diamonds has been removed. Each player stakes an agreed number of counters (preferably four, or some multiple of four) and the dealer stakes double that number. The players may divide their stakes between the four luxury cards in any manner they please. The cards are then dealt out one by one to each player, with an extra hand (as in Pope Joan) to create a corresponding number of 'stops'. Cards left over are given to the dummy. There is no trump suit. The object of the game is for a player to exhaust his cards as quickly as possible.

The player on the dealer's left leads. He may lead any suit he pleases, but of that suit he is obliged to lead the lowest (Ace ranking low) and he names the card as he plays it. The holder of the next highest card of the same suit plays and names it and so on until a 'stop' is reached. The player of the stop then leads to the next round. The game continues until one or other of the players is 'out', i.e. has played all his cards, at which he receives from all the other players one counter for each card left in their respective hands.

Whenever, during the course of the game, a card corresponding with one of the luxury cards is played, the player takes all the counters staked upon it. The general method of play and the division of any unclaimed stakes are the same as in the game of Pope Joan.

Spinado or *Spin:* (3–7 players) Spinado is closely related to New-market and is, therefore, another member of Pope Joan's family. It is played without a board and has only three pools, Matrimony, Intrigue and Game (or 'First Out'). To these, the dealer contributes two dozen counters – a dozen to Matrimony, half-a-dozen to Intrigue and half-a-dozen to First Out. The other players each contribute three counters only, all of which are placed in the First Out pool.

With the four twos and the eight of Diamonds removed from the pack, the cards are dealt round, with a dummy hand as in Pope Joan. In this game there is no 'turn up'. Matrimony is formed by King and Queen of Diamonds, Intrigue by the Queen and Knave of Diamonds. The Ace of Diamonds is known as Spinado, or more shortly, 'Spin'.

The player to the left of the dealer leads, and the holders of the next highest cards in the suit play them in succession until a stop is reached, when the last player leads for a new round. The holder of Spinado, when he plays, has the option of playing it with his own card and if he does so he makes his card a 'stop'. Thus, if he is playing to the six of Spades and he has the seven, he will say, 'Seven and Spin'. This makes the seven of Spades a stop. For this the Spinado holder receives three counters from each of the other players and the lead passes to him.

The holder of Spinado is not bound to play it with his first card, indeed it may be well to his advantage not to do so. Thus, suppose a ten of Clubs led and the holder of Spinado has the Knave and King of Clubs. It would be most unwise to play Spin with the Knave, for if the Knave proved to be a stop anyway, then Spin is wasted, and if any other player follows with the Queen, the King (which is a stop) can follow that. A good player,

117

therefore, would play up to this point without declaring Spin, then play out any known stops, and finally some card which he does *not* know to be a stop together with Spin, thereby still retaining the lead. By this means he will probably be First Out and become entitled to all the counters on that pool as well as a counter for each card left in the other hands.

On the other hand, it is not safe to keep Spin back for too long, for a player holding it when one of his opponents is First Out is bound to pay the winner double i.e. two counters for every card he is left with. The holder of the King of Diamonds receives two counters from each player, when he plays it. If he plays both the King and Queen of Diamonds he also takes the Matrimony pool. Any person playing Queen and Knave of Diamonds takes the contents of the Intrigue pool. If the same person holds (and plays) all three cards, he takes the counters in both pools. The player of a King, other than of Diamonds, receives one counter from each of the other players. First Out takes the counters from that pool and is exempt from contributing to the following pool unless, of course, he happens to be the dealer.

Matrimony: (5–14 players) This is an old-fashioned family game that may still afford a pleasant evening, especially among young people. It can be played by any number of persons from five to fourteen, and generally speaking, the more the merrier. The only equipment necessary, apart from one pack of cards, is a good-sized piece of cardboard or paper on which is drawn the following lay-out:

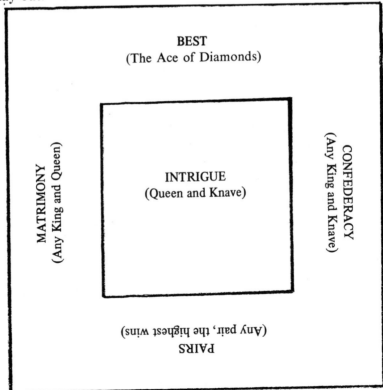

The lowest card cut determines deal and the first business of the dealer is to place his stake on each or on any of the chances, i.e. Best, Matrimony, Intrigue, etc. The other players, if they choose, then stake against the dealer on the chance or chances of their fancy. Each player's total stake must be at least one counter *less* than that of the dealer, so if the dealer stakes a total of nine no individual player may stake more than eight.

After this, the dealer gives two cards to each player, face down, starting with the player on his left. He then deals one more card to each player *face up*. If one of these cards is the Ace of Diamonds then the player receiving it 'sweeps all', that is he takes up all the stakes on the board. In this case, the cards are gathered in and reshuffled and a new round begins. If the Ace of Diamonds is *not* turned up, each player shows his hand and any of them having any of the five chances in their hand take all the stakes on that point. When two or more players happen to have a similar combination, the eldest hand takes precedence; should any chance not be gained it is left to stand over to the next pool. The Ace of Diamonds only 'sweeps all' if 'turned up'. If held in the hand it wins the chance marked 'Best', otherwise it ranks the same as any other Ace – as one of a pair for instance, to win the chance marked 'Pairs'. Should the Ace of Diamonds not appear at all, then the King, Queen or next highest card in that suit wins 'Best'. The deal must pass to the left at the end of every round.

All Fours: Known in America as Old Sledge or Seven Up, this game is usually played by two or four players with a full pack of cards which rank in play as in Whist. The game is played for seven points.

There are four different items which count towards the score, whence the name All Fours. These items are as follows:

HIGH: The highest trump out, scoring one to its original holder.

LOW: The lowest trump out, scoring one to its original owner.

KNAVE: The Knave of trumps, scoring one to the dealer, if turned up; otherwise one to the winner of the trick in which it falls.

GAME: Scoring one to the holder of the more valuable cards (trumps or otherwise) in the tricks won by him, according to the following scale.

For each ten	10
For each Ace	4
For each King	3

| For each Queen | 2 |
| For each Knave | 1 |

N.B. In the case of both the players scoring the point for game
or of neither party holding any card which counts towards game,
the elder hand scores the point.

TWO-HANDED ALL-FOURS

The players cut for deal. The dealer gives six cards to each,
turning up the thirteenth card as trump. If the elder hand is dissatisfied with his cards, he may say, 'I beg', in which case the
dealer is bound either to allow him (by the phrase 'take one') to
score one point, or to give each player three more cards from the
pack, turning up that next following by way of a fresh trump
card. If this should be of the same suit as the original trump, the
dealer is bound to give three more cards to each, again turning
up the seventh, until a new suit does actually turn up. If the
turn-up card is a Knave, the dealer scores one, this taking
precedence over any other score. If, by reason of the elder hand
'begging', there is a further deal, and the dealer a second time
turns up a Knave, he again scores one. The elder hand leads any
card he pleases. His opponent may choose to follow suit *or* trump.
If he cannot do either, he throws away. If he has a card of the
suit led and neither follows suit nor trumps, he becomes liable
to the penalty of the revoke, as will be explained.

In scoring, the order of precedence is High, Low, Knave,
Game, as shown above, subject to the contingency of Knave
having been the turn-up card, the point for this being scored
before the hand is played.

The play is mainly directed towards capturing the Knave, and
such cards as may score towards Game.

Some players score a point whenever the opponent does not
follow suit or trump. Some, again, make it the rule that each
player must count his score without looking at his tricks under
penalty of losing one or more points, as may be agreed, in the
event of a miscalculation. It should be arranged beforehand which
rules are to be followed.

FOUR-HANDED ALL-FOURS

The players cut to decide who shall be partners – the two highest
playing against the two lowest and facing each other as at Whist.
The right to the first deal is decided by the cut, the highest dealing. Afterwards the players deal in turn.

The dealer and the elder hand alone look at their cards in the
first instance, the option of begging resting with the latter. The
other two players must not take up their cards till the dealer has

decided whether he will 'give one' or 'run the cards' for a new trump. The players play in succession as in Whist. In other respects the play is the same as in the two-handed game.

Brag: (4–8 players) Brag is the parent of Poker and is one of the oldest of English card games. There are two versions, Single Brag and Three Stake Brag. Both are played with a full pack of cards. The Ace of Diamonds, Knave of Clubs and nine of Diamonds, known as 'braggers', are in effect Jokers, that is they are allowed to stand for any other card at the pleasure of the holder. The other cards rank as in Whist.

In Single Stake Brag the dealer starts by putting up any stake up to the agreed limit and then deals three cards, singly, to each player. Each player in turn looks at his cards and either 'brags' (puts up a stake equal to that of the dealer) or passes (drops out of the game). Any player may raise the dealer's stake and, in any case, each player who stays in the game must put up as much as the highest stake or abandon his hand, thus losing any stake he may have placed up to then. If no one is willing to brag, the dealer receives a single counter from each of the other players remaining in the game and the deal passes to the left for the next round. Should any player brag a stake that no other player is willing to meet, then he takes the pool without having to show his hand. Any player who is 'called' or 'seen' by another must show his hand and the best hand takes the pool – the order of value of the hands being as follows:

1. Three Aces *natural* (i.e. one that contains no 'bragger', although the Ace of Diamonds here ranks as a natural Ace).

2. Three Aces, including one or two braggers.

3. Three Kings or other smaller cards in due order, the higher being preferred to the lower and between those of equal value, natural threes being preferred to those made with the aid of braggers.

4. Pairs from Ace downwards, with the same preference for naturals.

5. In default of any pair, the hand holding the best single card: the Ace of Diamonds ranking highest, after it any other Ace, and so on.

Between the holders of absolutely equal cards, the elder hand has preference.

In Three Stake Brag, three separate stakes are made at the outset by each player, the winning of each being determined in a different manner. Three cards are dealt to each player but the last card of each is dealt face up. The best card so dealt entitles

121

its holder to the first stake. The second stake becomes the property of the holder of the best brag hand, the game being fought out as in Single Brag. The third stake goes to the player whose cards when totalled are nearest thirty-one; Aces count as eleven and all court cards count ten. Any player whose cards fall short of that number may, if he wishes and in due turn, draw a card or cards from the pack in the hope of amending his point. If he overdraws he is out of the game.

Slobberhannes: (4 players) Why Slobberhannes, no one knows. The word does not even appear in the O.E.D. although being a game of some antiquity it has every right to do so.

The game is played by four people with a Piquet pack of 32 cards (an ordinary pack from which the twos, threes, fours, fives and sixes have been removed). The cards rank as at Whist; there are no partnerships and no trumps. The players cut for the *lead*, the highest card taking the lead and the player on his right dealing. Deal and play are the same as in Whist but the object of the game is to avoid taking the first or last trick or any trick containing the Queen of Clubs. The player who wins any of these loses one point; if he wins all three he loses a further point. One point is lost for a revoke.

The player leading has a good advantage for he is likely to hold a safe losing card with which he will lead. The other three players will follow with the lowest card possible except that if a player sees that he cannot avoid taking the trick, he will do so with his highest card to avoid winning a trick with it at a later stage. The following tricks apart from the last one, may be won without damage, so long as the dreaded Queen of Clubs is not among them, and the players will use these to get rid of their high cards. The great interest of this game lies in the problem of not being left with the Queen of Clubs and it will soon be appreciated that the holders of the Ace and King of Clubs are in a very dangerous position until the Queen is out of the way. These three cards, therefore, are discarded as soon as possible. The best card of any suit of which there are but a few remaining is a very bad card to lead as, being certain of winning, it offers the opportunity for one or more of the three highest Clubs to be discarded.

Sift Smoke: (2–8 players) A complete pack of cards is divided into two halves, one portion being dealt to the players and the other remaining in the centre of the table. The player receiving the last card of the deal names its suit as trumps. The cards rank as at Whist. The tricks are of no value but each player must follow the suit led or play a trump. For each trick gained the player takes a card from the undealt portion and adds it to his hand and he who can hold out the longest wins the round.

Catch the Ten or *Scotch Whist:* This game may be played by any number from two to eight. The pack used consists of 36 cards, the twos, threes, fours and fives being removed. It is important that the cards should deal round equally. To ensure this, if there are five or seven players one of the sixes is also removed. With eight, all the sixes are removed, that is the game is played with the 32 card Piquet pack.

If the party consists of two, three, five or seven, each plays on his own account. Four play in partnership, as at Whist. Six players may either play three against three, or in three couples, each couple playing against the two others. Eight may play either four against four or in four independent partnerships, each pair against the other three. Partners and adversaries sit alternately.

Even where two only play, the cards are so dealt as to give three separate hands to each, all of which are played independently. In like manner, if three play, two hands are dealt to each. Dealing is by one card at a time, the last card being turned up by way of trump.

The cards, other than trumps, rank as at Whist. In the trump suit the Knave takes precedence, the order being Knave, Ace, King, Queen, ten, nine, eight, seven, six.

Game is forty-one points. The object of the game is to secure the tricks containing certain cards which have a special scoring value, as follows:

Knave of trumps . . . . 11 points
Ten of trumps . . . . 10 points
Ace of trumps . . . . 4 points
King of trumps . . . . 3 points
Queen of trumps . . . . 2 points

In addition to these, the players score for 'cards' i.e. for all cards they take in excess of their numerical proportion of the pack. Thus, if four be playing, their quota would be nine cards each. If the players on one side secure seven tricks (28 cards) they are ten in excess of their quota and score ten accordingly for cards.

The play follows the rules of ordinary Whist, but the special object of the game is to 'catch the ten' as it makes practically a difference of twenty to the score. The Knave is an even better card, but, being the leading trump, it necessarily remains with the side who received it by the deal.

Thirty-One (the German *Schnautz*): is a simple and lively card game for any number of persons. The full pack is used and the cards rank as at Whist.

The players, having put an agreed stake in the pool, each receive three cards dealt face down. Three additional cards are dealt face up in the middle of the table. The players, beginning with the elder hand, draw one card each from the hand in the middle of the table, replacing it with a discard from their own hand which is also left face up.

The primary object of the game is to hold three cards of the same suit which shall, added together, make 'thirty-one' – the ace counting eleven, court cards ten each and the other cards according to their nominal value. Obviously the desired number can only be made by an ace and two 'ten' cards. Next in scoring value to thirty-one is a triplet – between two or more triplets, the higher has preference. Triplets count thirty and a half and therefore override thirty. In default of thirty-one or a triplet, the highest total *in one suit* wins.

The discarding process continues until either one of the party makes thirty-one, in which case he shows his cards and claims the pool, or until some other player signifies by a knock on the table that he is 'content' (with his hand, that is). Should this occur, each of the other players (but not he who knocked) has a right to exchange one more card, after which the hands are shown, and the highest takes the pool.

5 Marbles

THERE ARE many versions of this very old game and the mastery of all of them depends on the skill of 'shooting' the marble. No rules exist as to how the marble should be propelled but the only accurate way of doing so is known as 'fulking'. The marble to be shot is placed just above the joint of the thumb of the right hand and held there by the tip of the forefinger, the top of the thumb being firmly grasped by the middle finger. Aim is then taken and the thumb let fly with enough force as to shoot the marble with the required speed. With practice sufficient skill may be obtained to hit another marble at several feet distance. In discharging the marble great care should be taken to keep the hand perfectly still. The forefinger should rest on the floor.

As the majority of marbles games need a good stretch of space free from obstacles, I give here three versions that are suitable for playing indoors.

Bridge-Board or *Arch-Board:* For this game a narrow piece of cardboard, about 14 inches by 1½ inches, is required. In this nine arches are cut, each being about an inch in height and about three-quarters of an inch wide. Another piece of cardboard or a piece of wood should be attached to the back of the strip to make it stand up. Over each arch a number is written, these numbers being at the discretion of the players, but no number over eight is allowed. The lower numbers should be in the middle of the bridge and the higher ones at the two sides. A good arrangement for beginners is 3 3 2 1 0 1 2 3 3.

One player is made the first bridge-keeper and the rest shoot their marbles from a line about four feet from the bridge. Every marble that fails to go through a hole is paid to the bridge-keeper, but for every successful shot the bridge-keeper pays the corresponding number of marbles to the shooter. As the position of bridge-keeper is usually a lucrative one, it is best changed at every round.

Bounce Eye: A circle, about a foot in diameter, is drawn on the ground; in a carpeted room, a circular piece of paper of the same size may be used. Each player contributes one marble towards the pool and these marbles are formed into a group in the middle of the circle. The players then take it in turns to stand over the ring and after taking aim let a marble fall into the pool. Expert 'fulkers' will use that method of propelling the marble in order to give its fall more force. If as a result of the latter operation, any marbles are driven out of the circle they are taken up by the player. If no marbles are driven out, the aimed marble becomes part of the pool which is then reformed in the middle of the ring.

Knock-Out or *Lag-Out:* Any number of players may join in this game. From a line about six feet from the wall, each player in turn 'fulks' a marble against the wall so that it rebounds. When a marble on the rebound strikes some other marble *all* the marbles on the floor become the property of the successful thrower. Any marble that rebounds beyond the throwing line is placed half-way between the throwing line and the wall.

Hairry My Bossie: This is a game of chance for two players. One player puts a number of marbles (about 1–5) into the hollow of his closed hand and says, 'How many?' In some parts of the country the phrase, 'Hairry my bossie' (hairry = rob; bossie = wooden bowl) is used. The other answers, 'Knock him down', upon which the player holding the marbles puts closed hands on his knees and continues to strike them up and down on his knee in order to give his opponent some idea of the number. He then says, 'How many blows?' and gets the reply 'As many as goes'. A guess is then made. If the guess is correct the guesser wins the marbles. If it is incorrect the guesser has to make up the difference between the number guessed and the real number. The players play alternately.

6 Forfeits

STRICTLY SPEAKING, any player found guilty of a misdemeanour during the course of a parlour game should, as a punishment, give up to the forfeit-master one of his or her personal belongings – a key, a handkerchief, a coin, a brooch, etc., then, towards the end of the proceedings, the forfeit-master should hold up these objects one by one, saying the following couplet:

> I have a thing and a very pretty thing,
> And who is the owner of this very pretty thing?

The owner of the object, in order to regain his possession, claims it and in return is compelled to perform a task, either ridiculous or seemingly impossible (or both), although sometimes it may be tolerably pleasant. There follows a selection from the hundreds of different 'forfeits' exacted by Victorian forfeit-masters.

128

In a large party the business of confiscating and then redeeming personal objects may be too lengthy and in such circumstances a selection of the following forfeits could be written on separate slips of paper and each enclosed in an envelope. As each penalty is earned, the name of the defaulter is inscribed on an envelope. Some of the punishments take only a few seconds to inflict. Others are as long and involved as the games which produced them and they may even involve the awarding of further forfeits. The time to be allowed at the end of the party for the playing out of the forfeits should be kept in mind when the selection of them is being made. If some of the more involved and amusing forfeits are to be enacted, it is a good idea to restrict the awarding of penalties to only a few of the games.

a. GENERAL FORFEITS

The Deaf Man: The individual who is punished with deafness is made to stand in the middle of the room and to answer three questions with the words, 'I'm deaf; I can't hear.' The fourth time he is addressed, however, he must say 'I can hear' and must do whatever is asked of him. The fun, to all but the penitent, is to make the first three proposals agreeable ones – such as bringing him a lady to kiss, to which command, of course, he must turn his deaf ear. The second offer might be that of a thousand pounds which again he cannot hear. The fourth communication is, of course, an unpleasant one for him. He may be asked to take the same lady to be kissed by another gentleman, to sing a comic song, dance a hornpipe, etc. This fourth command he must obey.

The Dummy: This consists in executing all acts of penitence ordered by other members of the party without uttering a word.

To Perform the Parrot: The penitent taking the part of the parrot must approach each person in the company, or, if there are too many present, any specified number. He or she must ask, 'If I were a parrot, what would you have me say?' and must then repeat the answer in a parrot voice. If the parrot is a lady, one gentleman – but one only – may have her say, 'Kiss your pretty Poll', and pretty Poll must say this and then submit to her own request.

Three Questions: The victim must leave the room while three questions are devised to which he must answer either 'yes' or 'no' without knowing what they are until *after* he has answered them.

Show the Spirit of Contrary: Whatever the player is told to do, he must do just the opposite.

The Living Statue: The victim must stand on a chair or stool and adopt the pose of any personality the company choose.

Make a Perfect Woman: This forfeit is a charming one. The player must select from the ladies present the personal features or traits that he most admires in each. In this way he has the opportunity of paying compliments to all the ladies, although, of course, the task requires great tact.

Give Good Advice: The player gives every member of the company what he considers to be a piece of good advice.

Make Your Will: The victim goes from player to player telling each one what he will receive as a legacy. To a bald man he may leave his hair, to another his common sense, to another his good looks, etc.

Blind Man's Waltz: A forfeit to punish a lady and a gentleman. They are both blindfolded and must waltz together.

The Cordial Greeting: A double forfeit. Two players are blindfolded and placed in opposite corners of the room. They must then find each other and, if a lady and a gentleman, must kiss. If two gentlemen they must approach one another, arms outstretched, meet and shake hands.

Ennui: The player must yawn until he makes someone else yawn.

Nose and Ears: The wrongdoer is required to grasp his left ear with his right hand and his nose with his left hand. He must then uncross his hands, slap his knees and reverse his original position i.e. grasp his right ear with his left hand and his nose with his right. This must be done *rapidly* many times in succession. Unless he is an accomplished artist at this movement the player will do little more than make gestures that promote much mirth.

Stiff as a Stake: The penitent must lie full length on the floor and cry in imploring tones, 'Here I lie, stiff as a stake, who'll come and save me for pity's sake!' To release a lady, a gentleman must kiss her and help her to her feet. To release a gentleman, one of the ladies must pull his hair and try to prevent him from rising.

Kiss Your Own Shadow: A gentleman thus condemned has a cunning way out. He arranges for his shadow to fall on the face of a lady and *then* he kisses it.

Blind Dancers: If the end of a party is nigh and there are still many forfeits to be redeemed, those left to do penance may all be blindfolded and compelled to go through the motions of whatever is the popular dance of the day. This collective punishment (which sometimes threatens to become a massacre) makes a good finale to any party.

b. SHORT AND TRICK FORFEITS

Call Your Sweetheart's Name up the Chimney

Laugh in One Corner of the Room, Cry in Another, Sing in Another and Dance in Another

Put Four Chairs in a Row, Take off Your Shoes and Jump Over Them: Even young ladies can perform this feat, for it is the shoes over which they jump.

Ask a Question to Which the Answer Cannot Possibly Be 'No': The question is, 'What does Y-E-S spell?'

Bite an Inch off a Hot Poker (or any other similar object): The secret is to hold the poker about an inch *off* the face and then to take an imaginary bite.

Lie Down on the Floor and Rise with Your Arms Folded

Put Yourself Through the Keyhole: The word 'yourself' should be written on a piece of paper and put through the keyhole.

Kiss a Book Inside and Outside Without Opening it: The book may be kissed inside the room and outside it.

Place a Book on the Floor so that No One can Jump Over it: The book is placed next to the wall.

Put One Hand Where the Other Cannot Touch it: On the elbow.

Constantinople: This absurd trick is included here because it was once the most popular of all forfeits. It was made even more absurd because everyone knew what was coming. The condemned player had to spell out the word 'Constantinople' as follows: 'C-o-n, Con; s-t-a-n, stan; t-i, ti,' at which point the rest of the players shouted, 'No, no!' implying that the victim had made a mistake.

Being Friendly: The player in default must walk around the room and bestow a friendly smile on every other person in turn.

c. KISSING FORFEITS

Opportunity (a double forfeit for a lady and gentleman): The couple must go into a corner of the room and spell aloud together the word 'Opportunity'. If, in ignorance of the joke, the couple do not kiss while they have the opportunity *instead* of spelling the word there is much laughter at their expense and they are rewarded with a further punishment. This, of course, should be another kissing forfeit.

The Beggar: This is an unusual punishment in that its ending is a happy one for the wrongdoer. The penitent approaches a lady and falls on his knees before her, imploring charity. She, touched by his distress, asks him: 'Do you want bread?', 'Do you want water?', 'Do you want a penny?', etc. To all these questions the beggar shakes his head impatiently. At length the lady must say 'Do you want a kiss?'; at this the beggar jumps up and accepts the offer.

The Sulks: This is a punishment awarded to ladies only. The lady paying the forfeit is ordered to sulk. This she does after whispering into the ear of the Forfeit Master the name of a gentleman on whom she would like to bestow a kiss. The Forfeit Master then presents the gentlemen to her one by one, making sure that the one of her choice is well at the back of the queue. As they are presented the lady turns her back on them all, in a sulky, pouting manner, until the arrival of the fortunate one of her choice to whom she offers, and from whom she receives, a kiss.

Languishing: This is another forfeit in which the wrongdoer comes off best, and the punishment descends on an innocent. The penitent is ordered into a corner to languish. This he does by simply going there and saying, 'I languish'. He is then asked, 'For whom do you languish?' and he answers by naming any player of the opposite sex to come and kiss him. The lady then languishes for a gentleman, who approaches her, kisses her and languishes for another lady, and so on until all the players have been called from their places, and form a line of ladies and gentlemen placed alternately. When the line is complete, the original languisher turns around and walks along the line kissing all the ladies. The lady left at the top does the same to all the gentlemen – and so on, down to the last player, who, having no one to kiss, has every reason to languish.

To Make a Wallflower of Oneself: If a lady is to pay the forfeit, she must place herself with her back to the wall until she has been kissed twice, by two different gentlemen, each of whom she must herself ask to come and kiss her. If this forfeit falls upon a gentleman, he must place himself against the wall until any *one* lady takes compassion on him, and releases him with a kiss.

The Candelabra: This is a forfeit for gentlemen only. The miscreant, known as the 'candelabra', must give a handkerchief to another. Then, taking a light in his own hand he must conduct the other gentleman to a lady. The handkerchief-holder kisses the lady but the poor candelabra must not; he only has his lips wiped with his own handkerchief by his companion. They then proceed to the next lady, and so on round the room.

To Fish For a Kiss: This is a forfeit for ladies only. A grape, or plum or the like, is tied to a piece of thread and suspended from a pen or pencil to resemble a fishing-rod. Any gentleman then approaches the lady and dangles the bait near her lips. She is compelled under the terms of the forfeit to take the bait in her teeth and must not let it go. Having thus hooked his fish, the angler then leads her round the room saying, 'See what a fine fish I have hooked!' He then detaches the rod, and taking the line up into his own mouth, he gradually approaches the lady until, inevitably, their lips meet. At this he gives her a kiss.

Three Kissing Questions: The forfeiter is sent out of the room while the remainder of the company try to devise three questions that will ensure some kissing by their answers. The forfeit holder must answer 'yes' or 'no' to these questions *before* knowing what they are. The questions might be:

1. Would you like to be kissed by every gentleman (or lady) in the room?
2. Would you like (so-and-so) *not* to kiss you?
3. Would you like (so-and-so) to kiss you?

To Run the Gauntlet: This is for a lady. The gentlemen range themselves in two lines to form an avenue. One of them then conducts the lady to the first gentleman who demands a kiss as price of passage; the avenue being thus opened, each gentleman tries to obtain a kiss before letting the lady pass but he must not step out of his place to get it; he may only stop her with his hands, but she may use any pretence she chooses, and also try to push her way through in order to pass without any kisses at all, or with only those she chooses to receive. If a gentleman moves out of his place to obtain a kiss, he, as a punishment, is condemned to stand in the middle of the room, with a lighted candle in each hand, until a lady releases him by kissing him.

To Give a Kiss à la Capuchin: This is a double forfeit for a lady and a gentleman. The lady and gentleman kneel back to back and mutually try to kiss each other by turning their heads.

To Choose From Three Actions: For a gentleman. A lady, whose identity is unknown to the wrongdoer, makes three gestures behind his back. A tap on the chin, a box on the ear and a kiss. He does not know in which order the gestures are made but must choose 'first, second or third'. Whichever he chooses he gets!

The Sofa: The penitent, on all fours, resembles a sofa, upon which a lady and a gentleman sit comfortably and exchange a kiss.

The Rabbit's Kiss: A double forfeit for a lady and gentleman. The couple kneel at a short distance from each other, holding the ends of about a yard of thread in their mouths. At a given signal they diminish the distance between them by drawing the thread into their mouths until their lips meet in a kiss.

Kissing a Nun: A double forfeit for a lady and gentleman. The couple kiss through the bars of the back of a chair.

The Pilgrim: A gentleman conducts a lady round the room saying to all the other gentlemen, 'A kiss for my sister, a morsel of bread for me'. To the ladies he says, 'A morsel of bread for my sister

135

and a kiss for me'. The bread is of no importance but the kisses are indispensable.

The Clock: The guilty party stands before the mantelshelf and calls a player of the opposite sex. The person called asks the clock what time it is. The clock replies whatever hour he or she likes and receives the same number of kisses.

The Hobby Horse or *Ariadne's Leopard:* The penitent, on his hands and knees, is obliged to carry around the room, seated on his back, a lady whom all the gentlemen (the penitent excepted) are privileged to kiss by turn.

The Kiss of Chance: The owner of the forfeit takes the four Kings and the four Queens from a pack of cards, shuffles them and deals them to four ladies and four gentlemen. Whoever has the King of Hearts kisses the one who has the Queen of Hearts and so on. He who has dealt merely watches. This is his punishment.

I'm in a Well: The victim must stand with his back to the wall, then choose a partner who stands facing him. This partner then chooses another partner of the opposite sex to stand with his back to her, and so on until all the company are standing in pairs in this way. On choosing his partner the victim must say, 'I'm in a well', to which someone must ask, 'How many feet deep?' The answer may be any number up to ten. He is then asked 'Whom will you have to pull you out?' and the one named stands next to him. When all have chosen a partner and are in position, each couple turns around so that No. 2 faces No. 3, No. 4 faces No. 5 and so on leaving No. 1 facing the wall. Then all the couples kiss each other as many times as the gentleman was feet in the well, but poor No. 1 is left to kiss the wall.

Second-hand Kisses: This penalty is inflicted upon a lady. She who is to perform it chooses a female friend. She then presents herself to a gentleman who kisses her, and she then has to carry the kiss to her companion. This performance is repeated as many times as there are gentlemen in the company.

Kiss the Lady You Love Without Anyone Knowing It: If the victim is in the know, he will kiss *all* the ladies in the room including, of course, the one he most admires.

Kissing Forfeits

Kneel to the Wittiest, Bow to the Prettiest and Kiss the One You Love: They must *not* be one and the same, and this makes the task fraught with perils.

Postman's Knock: This is a game in its own right which is often used as a forfeit. The instructions for play are on p. 50.

Index of Games

139